What's
Brand

Matthew Wharmby
and James Whiting

CAPITAL HISTORY

ISBN 978 1 85414 453 9

Published by
Capital History
www.capitalhistory.co.uk

Printed in the EU

Introduction

Have you ever wondered how a famous household brand got its name? We, the authors of this book, have and so we researched the names of over 250 well known brands to satisfy our – and hopefully your – curiosity.

From Asda and Aldi to Zanussi and Zara, we look at names that have been in or on shops either for many years or from only recent times. The only qualification is that they all have something of interest to write about. Reflecting the on-line age, you will also find names like Alexa, Cortana and Siri. There is plenty of material here for your next pub quiz.

While we couldn't include every brand name that exists, you should find in this book almost all of those you may think of looking up – so long as they are in current use. Made-up names got the highest priority for inclusion; pre-existing words a lower priority. There were only a handful we had to give up on, where the origin of the name had been lost even to the company owning the brand.

In researching the book, invaluable help has been provided by the companies' own websites and personnel within the companies. The book was possible only with their assistance. All trade marks are the property of the companies to which they are registered and we are grateful for being able include some in this book along with some vintage adverts.

Matthew Wharmby
James Whiting

An Aero advert from 1937.

Adidas combined the nickname and surname of German shoemaker Adolf "Adi" Dassler, who with his brother Rudolf developed lightweight running shoes, a pair of which were used by Jesse Owens in the 1936 Berlin Olympics. The brothers' subsequent falling out post-World War 2 prompted Rudolf to establish his own athletic shoe firm, Ruda, the name derived from his own nickname, and this became Puma, still a major competitor to Adidas.

AEG stands for *Allgemeine Elektricitäts-Gesellschaft*, which is German for 'General Electricity Company'. AEG was founded in 1887 in Berlin by Emil Rathenau, beginning with a few patents he had bought from the American inventor Thomas Edison. The first products made under the AEG brand were electric light bulbs. Today the company is part of the Electrolux Group.

Aero was launched by Rowntree in October 1935 and got its name from the air bubbles for which it is known, though the Greek word means 'of the sky'. Initially it was available only in the North of England, distribution expanding throughout the UK the following year. By 1936 Aero had reached New York. It was one of the first products promoted by Rowntree primarily on the strength of the brand, rather than the company name.

Aga stands for *Aktiebolaget Gas Accumulator*, the name of a Swedish company that invented a system of safe storage for the acetylene gas used in lighthouses. One of its staff - a Nobel prizewinning physicist - invented the famous cooker in 1922. Blinded in a terrible accident, he was convalescing at home when he realised his wife was using a range that was dangerous, dirty and exceptionally time consuming. He wanted to create a cooker that was instead clean, economical to run, easy to use and which produced good food with the minimum fuss. The AGA was an immediate success and came to Britain in 1929.

Aldi is a German supermarket chain and the name Aldi is short for Albrecht-Discount (in its anglicised form). Its very first shop was opened by the Albrecht brothers Karl and Theo in the German city of Essen in 1913. The company started trading in the UK in 1990 with the opening of its first English shop at Stechford, Birmingham.

Alexa The engineers at Amazon wanted to replicate the computer in *Star Trek* which always answered when any *Star Trek* crew simply called out the word "computer," says David Limp, the vice president in charge of Amazon Devices. The challenge was to choose a word that people didn't ordinarily use in everyday life, so "Computer" wouldn't work. After testing various names the team selected the name Alexa. The engineers also liked the name because of the hard X sound in the middle, making pronunciation clearer for the system to recognise, and because it was 'a little reminiscent of the Library of Alexandria' which was at one time the keeper of all knowledge.

Alka-Seltzer was introduced in 1931, primarily as an antacid for stomach discomfort and heartburn. The Alka is short for alkaline and Seltzer means effervescent water.

Alpen is German for the Alps. A senior Weetabix executive was enjoying a family skiing holiday in Switzerland when he discovered a weird and wonderful breakfast created for him. He was impressed with how it kept him going on the slopes and he brought the recipe back to England. Launched in 1971, it was the UK's first Swiss muesli.

Amazon Initially, Amazon founder Jeff Bezos called his e-commerce company (at that point just a bookseller) Cadabra Inc. The name was short for 'abracadabra' to imply how magical he felt online shopping would be. But after a lawyer misheard the name as 'cadaver,' Bezos had further thoughts. A bit of brainstorming led Bezos to relentless.com, which he and his wife were very keen on. Friends told him Relentless sounded pushy and unfriendly, but Bezos still bought the domain name in 1994. If you type relentless.com into your browser, you'll go straight to the amazon.com homepage. The same applies to browse.com and awake.com, two other names Bezos considered. He also came up with the name Aard so as to be top of alphabetical lists. Before the days of Google's complex algorithms some search engines would arrange links alphabetically, so having an 'A' name would be a definite advantage. Finally, Bezos settled on Amazon. He could still keep his company at the top of the alphabet, the name sounded like 'amazing' and borrowing the name of the world's longest river evoked how huge he wanted it to be.

An Alka-Seltzer advert
from the 1950s.

Ambrosia – best known for creamed rice pudding – was founded in Devon in 1917 by Albert Morris, whose initials formed the basis of the trade name, a word associated with the food of the Greek gods, he chose for the milk products sold by his creamery.

Andrex was first manufactured in 1942 at St Andrew Mill in Walthamstow, but was originally intended as a disposable handkerchief before the name was adopted for its two-ply toilet tissue. Now owned by Kimberley-Clark, the company became famous for its TV adverts featuring a rambunctious Labrador puppy trailing a roll of its signature toilet paper.

Android The word Android is a generic name for a robot patterned after man and was in existence about 1000 years ago. It is formed by the Greek words *andro* meaning man and *eides* meaning 'form or shape.' In the 12th century St Albertus Magnus created an automaton which looked like a human and called it Android.

Aol in its initial capitalised form stood for America On Line, but early expansion of the company's Internet services beyond the USA brought the acronym into more popular and then official use. Its growth was so swift that the company purchased TimeWarner in 2001, but there was a decline thereafter.

Aon insurance was known from its post-first world war foundation in Detroit until 1987 as the prosaic Combined Registry Co., selling health and accident insurance and growing steadily in the process. As Aon, the name evoking the permanence of aeons, expansion came rapidly and to multiple overseas territories, moving into outsourcing and human resources, but in Britain, where the group has been headquartered since 2012, the name has been best known on Manchester United shirts.

Apple was founded in 1976 by Steve Jobs and Steve Wozniak, giving its name to its first desktop computer, from which an almost inexhaustible stream of innovative products followed in spite of Jobs's enforced absence from the company for several years. Its rise to trillion-dollar status is well-documented. So far as the name is concerned, in the biography of Steve Jobs he told his biographer Walter Isaacson that he was on one of his fruitarian diets, had just returned from an apple farm and thought the name sounded "fun, spirited and not intimidating". Nine years earlier The Beatles had also chosen Apple as the name to be used for their own record label and commercial activities, their single "Hey Jude" being the first Apple record to appear in August 1968. A protracted legal dispute between members of the group and the computer company resulted in 2006 in the former agreeing not to enter the computer business and the latter agreeing not to enter the music business.

The Apple record label as introduced in 1968 by The Beatles.

Aquascutum From the Latin *aqua*, water, and *scutum*, shield, this name dates from 1851 when tailor and entrepreneur John Emary opened a menswear shop in London's Regent Street. The name was threatened with extinction in 2012 when the company fell into administration. It was bought from the administrators by a Chinese company which sold it to its present owners, another Chinese company, the Shandong Ruyi Group, in 2017.

Argos catalogue shops followed on from Green Shield trading stamps (1958-1973). The Argos company was founded in 1972 by Richard Tompkins who had previously established Green Shield trading stamps in the UK. Whilst on holiday in the Greek city of Argos, he came up with the idea that people could purchase goods from his Green Shield catalogues with cash rather than his savings stamps.

1978 US advert for
Apple Computers.

Arriva was perhaps the first instance of a deliberately meaningless Euro-name being chosen to adorn the disparate international operations of a large company, in this case the former T. Cowie Ltd, which grew from a motorcycle dealer in Sunderland to a prestige London coach firm and then to bus and train operations. The corporate image was also all-encompassing and has since been updated with a new logo that, according to the company, symbolises "wheels within wheels".

Asda is an abbreviation of Asquith and Dairies, the two components of today's supermarket giant, a subsidiary since 1999 of Walmart. The Asquith family of Wakefield were butchers and their expansion from 1949 brought them into contact with dairy farmers, another general aspect of the cattle business. In 1965 Asquith merged with what had by then become Associated Dairies.

ASOS, the acronym for As Seen On Screen, was founded in 2000 and broke out of the box that defeated other early online fashion retailers by selling imitations of screen-worn items. Profitability was achieved in 2004 and the company never looked back, exploiting Twitter, Instagram and, most recently, mobile apps as new marketing mediums as soon as they came out.

Audi is Latin for 'listen' and the company name is based on the Latin translation of the German surname of the founder, August Horch, who set up his first car manufacturing company in 1899 in Cologne. In 1932 four companies, Audi, DKW, Horch and Wanderer joined together to form Auto Union AG. The amalgamated company, which kept the name Audi, needed a new logo, which is how the four interlocking rings were born.

Aviva, not to be confused with Arriva, is the trading name of Norwich Union, the long-established insurance agent until its merger in 2000 with CGU. Expansion since then has been global, encompassing pensions, commercial insurance and fund management as well as its long-term sponsorship of Norwich football club in its traditional home region. Continuity has been ensured through the retention of the yellow and green-based company graphics, and the name itself is a nod to the 'life' aspects of its historic insurance policies.

B&Q are simply the initials of Richard Block & David Quayle, founders in 1969 of a shop in Southampton exploiting Britain's earliest forays into the DIY pastime (and that particular acronym stuck at much the same time as that of their own company). Expansion and acquisition brought B&Q to its current size in the UK before purchases of similar warehouse-sized outlets were made in Ireland, Poland and China, though some contraction has been evident in the past decade.

Batchelor's foods are named after William Batchelor, a former tea salesman, who began the canning company in Sheffield in 1895 to supply the home with tinned vegetables. Peas have always been one of the main vegetables associated with the firm and it was Batchelor who introduced the nation to tinned mushy peas.

Barclays traces its ancestry back to two goldsmith bankers, John Freame and Thomas Gould, who were doing business in Lombard Street, London in 1690. In 1736, Freame's son, Joseph took his brother-in-law James Barclay on as a partner, and his surname later became the name of the business. In 1967 Barclays Bank installed (at Enfield, north London) the world's first ATM.

Bata Shoes was founded in 1894 in what is today the Czech Republic by Tomáš Baťa. A large factory was set up in 1932 in East Tilbury to serve the British market and by the middle of that decade Bata had 4000 shoe shops throughout Europe. The East Tilbury factory closed in 2005 and although Bata shoes are still available in this country there are no longer any Bata shops in the UK. The company has its headquarters in Switzerland.

Beko was founded by Vehbi Koç and Leon Bejerano in Istanbul, Turkey in 1969. The company's name is a combination of the first two letters of the founders' surnames.

Ben & Jerry's This American ice cream company was founded in 1978 by Ben Cohen and Jerry Greenfield. With a $5 correspondence course in ice cream-making and a $12,000 investment, including a $4,000 loan, Ben and Jerry opened their first ice cream scoop shop in a renovated petrol station in Burlington, Vermont. Their ice cream, infused with eclectic flavours and names suggested by fans, began to be sold in the UK in 1994.

Benson & Hedges gained a Royal Warrant in 1878 after Richard Benson and William Hedges had fulfilled the supply of tobacco to the Royal Family for the statutory five years (the lack of demand for cigarettes among today's Royals has since caused the Royal Warrant to be revoked). A US branch was soon established and is now under the ownership of Philip Morris. The decline of smoking in recent years has put an end to the extensive motorsport sponsorship once enjoyed by the brand, and packets of cigarettes themselves must now display graphic pictures of the documented physical results of smoking rather than the manufacturers' brands or devices.

Bic Frenchman Marcel Bich had set up a business in 1944 making parts for fountain pens and mechanical pencils. With the rising popularity of ballpoint pens, he added plastic pen barrels to his repertoire. Then in 1950, he decided to try his hand at making his own full pens. Bich acquired a patent licence from ballpoint pen inventor Laszlo Biro and did everything to find the ideal ink formula and the perfect fitting between ball and ink, using machines of extreme precision from Swiss clock making. These ones were simple without a retractable tip, and cost a lot less than other pens. Luckily, Bich decided to shorten his last name from Bich to Bic. In 1973 his company diversified into razors.

Bing is Microsoft's search engine, positioned from the outset as a competitor to Google but never quite able to muster enough support from its anodyne 'Microsoft Live Search' name until a study in 2009 came up with this short, easy to spell and recognisably onomatopoeic word. At one point it was going to be called Bang, but try using that as a verb!

Early can and advertising for Bird's custard.

Bird's custard contains no real birds, but it also contains no eggs, this being marketed from its inception as the pudding's major selling point. Birmingham chemist Alfred Bird, whose wife was allergic to eggs, created it in 1837 and gave his name to the company that began producing the immediately popular results. Bird's custard soon took powder form and has remained universally popular in Britain ever since, but in recent times the company has moved between several multinationals and suffered their own internal reorganisations, passing from General Foods to Philip Morris, then to Kraft Foods and now Premier Foods.

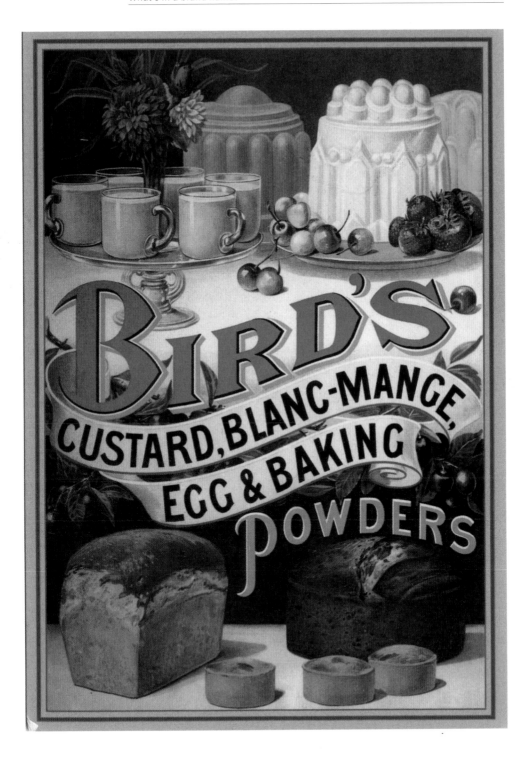

Bird's Eye is named after Clarence Birdseye, who founded the
frozen food company in America following his invention of a
fast-freezing method in 1924 that, unlike slow freezing, kept the
texture of the food intact and better retained its flavour. Frozen
foods using this new method began to be sold in America under
the Bird's Eye name in 1929 and in the UK in 1938. A year
earlier Smedley's had been the first company to introduce a
frozen food product to this country when it began to sell frozen
asparagus. Under General Foods Corporation, expansion to the
UK saw the creation of Birds Eye's best-known product, the fish
finger, in 1955.

Biro As mentioned in the paragraph about Bic, the biro
ballpoint pen owes its name to Laszlo Biro, a Hungarian, who
first demonstrated his pen at a trade fair in 1931. He obtained
a patent for his new pen in 1938. The first ballpoint pen had
been invented about 50 years earlier by a John J. Loud, but it
did not attain commercial success. If it had we might be using
Loud pens.

Bisto meat-flavoured gravy powder was introduced
in Britain in 1908. The name stands for 'browns, it
seasons and thickens in one'. Added to gravy to give
a richer taste and aroma, it quickly became a best
seller. The famous 'Ahh, Bisto' slogan was first used
in 1919 and is still in use over 100 years later.

Blomberg dates from 1883 when the company,
founded by Bernhard Blomberg, started operating in
the metallurgical industry. Gradually the company
left the business, established a distribution channel
for home appliances in 1935, and in 1949 started
producing washing machines.

BMW stands for *Bayerische Motoren Werke* (Bavarian Motor
Works). BMW was created in 1917 from the Munich firm Rapp-
Motorenwerke. The company was incorporated into Knorr-
Bremse AG in 1920 before being refounded as BMW AG in
1922. It was the successor of Bayerische Flugzeugwerke AG,
founded in 1916. 1916 is therefore considered by the company as
being BMW's founding year.

Body Shop Founded in 1976 by the late British environmental and human rights campaigner Dame Anita Roddick, The Body Shop started life as a small business in Brighton selling just 25 products. Roddick's emphasis was on ethically-sourced natural ingredients that had not been tested on animals. L'Oréal purchased the Body Shop in 2006 and sold it to Natura in 2019.

Boots, ironically, are probably the only thing you can't buy at the long-established British chemists (pharmacists in more accurate parlance). The name derives from John Boot, who in 1849 established a shop in Nottingham selling herbal remedies and passed it on to his wife upon his death; his son later greatly expanded the business into drug research and manufacturing. Related expansionary ventures have encompassed cycling, with the brief ownership of Halfords, and the Dollond and Aitchison firm of opticians. In recent years ownership has been in the hands of US pharmaceutical giant Walgreens.

Bosch In 1886 Robert Bosch set up an engineering workshop in Stuttgart. Bosch entered the world of domestic appliances by producing its first refrigerator at the Leipzig Spring Fair in 1930. The fridge had quite a small capacity compared with an electric fridge introduced by the General Electric Company in America three years earlier (in the UK, electric fridges were on sale in 1928 but were slow to catch on and 20 years later only two per cent of the population here had one). Bosch sold their first washing machines in 1952 and their first fully automatic washer-dryer in 1967. Today the company produces all manner of electrical domestic appliances.

Bovril was invented by a Scotsman, John Lawson Johnston, after he won a contract to supply one million cans of beef to the French army in the 1870s. The problem was, Britain didn't have enough meat so Johnston developed this product from beef extract and supplied it instead. It was introduced to the British public in the early 1880s and first sold as Johnston's Fluid Beef. It was rebranded Bovril in 1886, the first part of the name coming from Bovine – the Latin for Ox. The second part was inspired by the word Vril, the name given to a powerful energy-giving fluid in a popular occult novel of the time, *The Coming Race*. Often seen as a rival to Marmite, both brands are owned by Unilever.

BP is the familiar abbreviation and now pre-eminent brand
name for the British Petroleum Company, founded and still
headquartered in London. It developed from the Anglo-Persian
Oil Company (later the Anglo-Iranian Oil Company) exploiting
deposits in that country and changed its name to British
Petroleum in 1959. Its modern image uses green and yellow
colours extensively, first in a shield containing the BP letters,
which were then italicised and later replaced by today's sunburst.

Branston Pickle owes its name to the town in which it was
first mixed in 1922 by Crosse & Blackwell; Branston, in
Staffordshire. Despite the move of production to London it
became the company's signature product and today sells 17
million jars a year in the UK. Crosse & Blackwell no longer
appears on the jars, however. The company is now owned by
Mizkan following spells with Nestle and Premier Foods.

Early 20th century
Bryant & May
matchbox label.

Bryant & May Match-making company Bryant & May was
formed in 1843 by two Plymouth Quakers, William Bryant
and Francis May, to trade in general merchandise. Their first
order was for 720,000 matches. The following year they began
manufacturing candles and in 1861 the partners opened a large
factory in the London district of Bow to produce the matches for
which the company is best known. Closed in 1979, the building
still stands and is today flats.

BT is an abbreviation of British Telecom, itself shortened from
British Telecommunications plc, the identity of the United
Kingdom's state telephone operator upon its privatisation in 1984.

Burberry is well established as a major high fashion retailer with a strong and distinctive identity. It was founded in 1856 by Thomas Burberry, focusing initially on men's outdoor clothing only. In 1879 Burberry invented the gabardine raincoat, still produced by the company (and others) today and made from a tough, tightly-woven and water-resistant fabric of specially processed Egyptian cotton.

Burger King began in 1953 in Jacksonville, Florida as Insta-Burger King, a competitor to fast-food giant McDonald's but never quite approaching the latter's market dominance. At one point the company was British-owned via Grand Metropolitan's takeover of Pillsbury (of the famous Doughboy) in 1988. In Australia the restaurants are known as Hungry Jack's.

Make the day with Cadburys Milk Tray

A mid-1950s advert.

Cadbury, quintessentially British but more recently American-owned and with production moved to Poland, was founded in 1824 by John Cadbury. He and subsequent generations of the Cadbury family were widely admired for instituting progressive working conditions, including the foundation of a model village for its workers, Bournville, near Birmingham. Little introduction is needed to the myriad of delicious chocolate products produced there over most of the next two centuries, which would merit a book of their own!

Caffè Nero is simply the Italian for black coffee, the staple of the chain operated in England since 1997 and more recently running over a thousand branches worldwide.

Canon This Japanese camera and scanner company was originally named *Seikikōgaku Kenkyūsho*. In 1947 the company name was changed to the Canon Camera Company Inc, which was shortened to Canon Inc in 1969. The name Canon comes from Buddhist bodhisattva Guan Yin (pronounced Kannon in Japanese), whose thousand arms embrace all.

Carling The origin of Carling beers dates back to 1818, when Thomas Carling, an English farmer from Yorkshire, settled in Ontario, Canada, with his family. He brewed an ale there which he started selling in 1840 and then his sons, John and William, built a five-storey brewery in 1878 to expand the business. Carling beers were brought to Britain in 1952. An advertising slogan from the 1970s and 80s – 'I bet he drinks Carling Black Label' – became a bit of a catchphrase to refer to someone displaying strong masculine energy and had a significant effect on sales here. It is now owned by Molson Coors, formed by a merger of two well-known American and Canadian lagers.

Carlsberg is another popular beer that benefited from a strong advertising campaign, in this case with the perhaps less-than-true slogan 'Probably the best beer in the world'. The company that produces it dates back to 1847 when it was set up by Danish industrialist J C Jacobsen. Taking the name of his five-year-old son, Carl, and the Danish word for hill, 'bjerg' he built his new brewery on a hill just outside Copenhagen.

Carnation Milk owes its name to a brand of cigars. The tinned milk company began life as the Pacific Coast Condensed Milk Company in 1899. A few years after, while passing a tobacconist's window in Seattle, the firm's owner Elbridge Amos Stuart saw a display of 'Carnation' cigars and decided that the name would be good for his tinned milk. His company subsequently adopted the name Carnation Evaporated Milk Company. The company's resulting attention to breeding of healthy dairy cattle later resulted in the renaming of a cattle town near its base in Washington to Carnation.

Carnation advert from the 1930s.

Cartier, the high-end French jewellers, came into being under that name in 1847 when Adolphe Picard passed his Paris shop to apprentice Louis-François Cartier. Successive generations of Cartiers continued the quality and innovation aspect and contributed to the development and mass adoption of the wristwatch in the 20th century. In the 1960s the American and Paris branches were reunited under investment ownership and today there is still a family presence in the business.

Cerebos The origin of this made-up name, as used for a brand of salt, is uncertain although 'Ceres' is the Roman goddess of agriculture and grain. Cerebos salt was first sold in the UK in 1884 and had added calcium and magnesium to give it greater nutritional value and to help it flow more freely.

Chanel is the life's work of the inimitable Coco Chanel, Parisian socialite and designer whose personality and reputation pre-war, wartime and post-war carried her through all adversity. Basic millinery with what materials could be obtained amid perennial

shortages gave rise to the deliberate section of fabrics to exploit trends in fashion, whilst a side venture of commissioning a fragrance to accompany the 1921 collection was so successful that No.5 perfume built a worldwide brand all its own. After Coco Chanel's death, the company was revitalised under Karl Lagerfeld and remains an arbiter of fashion and style today.

Cif began life in this country in 1974 as Jif, which it still is in Australia, New Zealand, Japan, the Middle East and the Nordic countries. As people in some European countries have difficulty with the hard J, the name Cif was used in continental Europe and this name took over from Jif here in 2001 to standardise the name throughout Europe.

Clark's was founded in 1825 by Street, Somerset brothers Cyrus and James Clark. At first the business was in wool rug making, but the success of the slippers made from offcuts saw this aspect given greater prominence. Like the Cadbury family, the Clarks saw the welfare and education of their workforce as key to maintaining success, in this case impelled by Quaker values. In the 20th century, American manufacturing methods and the development of a standard system to measure children's feet saw the success of the lines of the tough school shoes worn by generations of British schoolchildren, including this author. Expansion into foreign markets in recent decades, particularly China, India and the USA, has been accompanied by the re-establishment of a manufacturing facility in England, coincidentally right back in Street where it all began.

Clipper tea was started in 1984 in a Dorset kitchen by a tea-obsessed husband-and-wife team. They wanted to share their love of great tea with a promise of ethical sourcing and natural production. The name refers to the tea clipper sailing vessels of the 19th Century. The story of the business began with just two chests of finest-quality Assam tea, sold to local health food shops and cafes. Today there are over 150 different Clipper products sold in over 50 countries. In 1994 Clipper became the UK's first Fairtrade tea company and today Clipper is the world's largest buyer of Fairtrade tea.

Coca-Cola famously had a very small amount of cocaine, hence the 'coca' part of the name, as one of its original ingredients when it first went on sale in Atlanta, Georgia in 1886. It was introduced as a temperance drink but needed something to give it some of the relaxing properties of alcohol. All traces of cocaine were removed from the drink by 1929. The first sales in the UK were in 1900 but the drink did not achieve volume sales here until the 1920s.

Colgate takes its name from William Colgate (1783-1857), who began a small business producing candles and soap in 1806. His son Samuel took over the Colgate Soap Company on the death of his father. Toothpaste, for which the company is best known, was introduced in tubes in 1896; it had produced 'aromatic' tooth cleaning powder since 1873.

Opposite: A Colgate advert from the late 1940s – very much of its time.

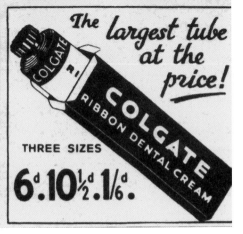

Colman's is the firm established by Jeremiah Colman in Norwich in 1814, to make mustard according to his recipe of combining brown mustard and white mustard, and passed the business down to his adoptive nephew. The company standards of yellow branding and bull's head logo were adopted early, and the same humanitarian principles as those that inspired Cadbury and Clark improved social welfare for the workforce. Along the way Colman's acquired competitors, but ownership has been in the hands of Unilever since 1995.

Cortana is named after a synthetic intelligence character with that name in Microsoft's Halo video game franchise, originating in Bungie game folklore.

Costa Coffee Italian Immigrant brothers Bruno and Sergio Costa founded a coffee roastery in Lambeth in 1971, supplying local caterers. The family had moved to England in the 1960s. Costa branched out to selling coffee in 1978, when its first store opened on Vauxhall Bridge Road, London.

Costco, the membership-based discount warehouse chain, began as Price Club (not just a concept but the name of the founder) in a former aircraft hangar in San Diego; former employees later expanded the idea to Seattle as Costco, and in 1993 Price Club and Costco merged, fending off attention from Walmart. In the UK the company has 29 locations.

Cow & Gate In 1881 Brothers Charles and Leonard Gates decided to go into dairy trade, naming their business 'The West Surrey Central Dairy'. They built their own creameries and sold their wares in little brown jugs featuring a picture of a cow looking through a gate. In 1908 the first adverts for Cow & Gate baby milk appeared in newspapers and in 1929. Following the product's success, the name was adopted to replace the company's original name. Today the company is owned by Danone.

Crest was the new name, from 1955, of an American toothpaste marketed as containing fluoride and thus initially known as Fluoristan. Under the ownership of Procter & Gamble then and now, the line has grown to twenty products. The origin of the name is not recorded.

Crosse & Blackwell In 1819, an existing provisions company named West & Wyatt was joined by two 15-year old apprentices, Edmund Crosse and Thomas Blackwell. In 1830 they borrowed £600 (around £70,000 at today's prices) from their families to buy the business, which then became Crosse & Blackwell. The company was one of the first to secure a Royal Warrant from Queen Victoria.

Currys PC World combines two long-established British high street electronics retailers, which together subsumed a third, Dixons. Henry Curry was originally a manufacturer of bicycles, setting up ship in Leicester in 1888. Electric goods became more popular over the years, and in 1984 the similar business of Dixons was acquired. The Dixons name was superseded by Currys in 2006, but the PC World identity was bolted on in 2015.

Daddies Sauce A Rossendale grocer by the name of Hammer Schofield had a small sauce kitchen at the rear of his premises. One day in 1899 while he was cooking some of his own recipe 'Daddies' brown sauce that he had just started to sell locally, he was visited by the owner of the Midland Vinegar Company, Edwin Moore, to whom he owed some money. Moore saw and smelled the sauce brewing and, clearly impressed, offered to cancel the debt as part of an offer to buy the recipe. A deal was done and Daddies Sauce went into volume production. It seems likely that Schofield's children nicknamed the brew Daddy's Sauce but this is not recorded.

Daim is the spelling adopted for the European market in 2005 for what was historically known in the UK as the Dime bar, an adaptation by Swedish company Marabou of the 'Heath Bar' sold in America. The brand subsequently passed to Kraft and was spun off by that concern as today's Mondelez conglomerate.

Dairylea was introduced in 1950 by the Kraft company. Despite the quintessentially English-sounding name this product has Belgian roots, the spreadable processed cheese being made in Namur. It was first sold only in round boxes of six foil wrapped triangular portions which quickly became popular, especially with children. Its name gives the air of a dairy set amidst open grassy land.

Danone was founded by medical doctor Isaac Carasso, who began producing yogurt in Barcelona in 1919. The brand was named Danone, which translates to 'little Daniel', after his son Daniel.

Dave is the irreverent and unmistakable moniker for a free-to-air television channel that until 2007 had laboured under the cumbersome title of UKTV G2. The name was chosen to reflect the fact that "everyone knows a bloke called Dave" and the channel was accordingly positioned to show carefree, laddish sort of programming. The resulting boost to viewership spawned a similarly cheekily-named catchup channel called 'Dave Ja Vu'.

Decca was established as a British record label in 1929 by stockbroker Edward Lewis after he bought a gramophone business from William S. Samuel. The name Decca had been coined by Samuel for his portable wind-up gramophone that had become a big success. The name was arrived at by merging the name Mecca with the initial D of his company's logo 'Dulcet'. Samuel, a linguist, chose Decca as a brand name because it was easy to pronounce in most languages. The name survives on CDs.

Del Monte In the 1870s and 1880s, California became a major producer of fruits and vegetables. In 1886 the Del Monte brand name was originally used in the 1880s by a Californian foods distributor to designate a premium blend of coffee prepared for the Hotel Del Monte on the Monterey peninsula.

DHL stands for Dalsey Hillblom Lynn. It is a German logistics company based in Bonn providing international shipping and courier services. Its name is derived from the initials of the last name of its founders; Adrian Dalsey, Larry Hillblom and Robert Lynn.

Diageo is the name invented by branding consultancy Wolff Olins to christen the merger of Guinness and Grand Metropolitan in 1997, a fusion that created the largest drinks manufacturer in the world. Its roots evoke the Latin *dies* (day) and the Greek *geo* (world) to emphasise the global nature of the company.

Diesel clothing began as Moltex, in which Italian designer Renzo Rosso bought shares in 1978; he cited American marketing, Italian creativity and German systems as his inspiration for success. The name evokes hard-wearing industrial clothing, but its denim jeans have been followed by multiple other lines for men and women, plus eyewear and watches, all advertised in an unusually surreal fashion. At the time the brand name was chosen, diesel was also viewed as an alternative form of energy, so for him the word also stood for an alternative taste in fashion. The brand's first flagship stores, in New York, Rome and London, opened in 1996.

Disney takes its name from its founders Walt and Roy Disney, who set up the Disney Brothers Cartoon Studio in 1923. Walt was always the more involved of the two brothers and it was Roy who suggested that the company be rebranded as the Walt Disney Studio early in its life. Today it is known as the Walt Disney Company and has a number of other brands under its wing including 20th Century Fox and Lucasfilm with the Star Wars films and valuable merchandising rights.

Domestos Wilfrid Handley, a dentist from Heaton, Newcastle, set up the Hygiene Disinfectant Company and, according to Unilever, in 1929 chose the brand name from the Latin *domus* meaning house and the Greek *osteon* meaning bone, suggesting 'backbone of the home'.

Doritos hail from a Mexican Spanish term meaning golden brown, and grew out of the popularity of fried tortillas sold at Disneyland. Frito-Lay began producing them and added flavours appealing to American palates, which even included an ambitious study that refined the shape and size of the individual pieces. They were one of the quintessentially American snack foods to penetrate the UK in the 1990s.

DPD stands for Dynamic Parcel Distribution. DPD began life in the UK in 1970 as Courier Express, changing its name to Parceline in 1984. La Poste bought the company in 2000 and in 2008 Parceline was renamed DPD. La Poste has invested substantially in DPD's infrastructure and the company claims to be the leader in pursuing carbon neutral parcel delivery.

Dr Martens came about by accident, quite literally, when German army doctor Klaus Märtens found that his Wehrmacht-issue jackboots wouldn't cushion the ankle he had injured skiing while on leave during the second world war. He used some tyres to create an air-filled sole and after the war went into business making shoes with surplus Luftwaffe rubber. Though German in origin, Dr Martens became a British fixture, the name being anglicised when Griggs bought the rights to manufacture the shoes in the UK in the 1960s; since then every imaginable subculture has taken to these sturdy and indestructible work boots.

Dr Pepper did actually exist but he was not the founder of the company making the carbonated soft drink of the same name. It was started in 1885, one year before Coca-Cola, by a pharmacist called Charles Alderton and, it is said, named after Dr Charles Pepper, the father of a girl he was fond of. It was first nationally marketed in the United States in 1904 and came to Britain later in the 20th Century.

Dulux first appeared as a brand name in 1931 with the launch of a new formulation paint by ICI that was longer lasting. The name was chosen to represent Durability (or alternatively US manufacturer DuPont, who inspired the paint) and Luxury and for a time was spelled DuLux.

Dyson In 1974, James Dyson bought a Hoover Junior vacuum cleaner, which he says lost suction over time. Frustrated, Dyson took it apart and found that its bag was clogging with dust, causing suction to drop. Dyson had recently built an industrial cyclone tower that separated paint particles from the air using centrifugal force. This gave him the idea for a vacuum cleaner designed on the same principle. Five years and 5,127 prototypes later he had invented the world's first bagless vacuum cleaner. The Dyson company was founded in Wiltshire in 1991 and other inventions by Dyson include the ball-mounted barrow and the Airblade hand dryer.

easyJet is just one of the 'easy' range of companies owned by Sir Stelios Haji-Ioannou; this particular undertaking is a low-cost airline founded in 1995 and operating out of Luton Airport, but other companies in the group, all employing a cheerful bright orange branding and Cooper Black font, are easyCar, easyBus, easyHotel, easyFoodstore, easyGym, easyProperty and easyCoffee.

eBay Starting up in 1995, originally this auction website belonged to the Echo Bay Technology Group, founder Pierre Omidyar's consulting firm. Omidyar had tried to register the domain name echobay.com, but found it already taken by the Echo Bay Mines, a gold mining company, so he shortened it to his second choice, ebay.com. In 1999 ebay.co.uk began operating in the UK. The first item sold on the site in this country was a CD by a German rock band.

Ecover In 1979, after seeing the damage to waterways and aquatic life caused by phosphates and other chemicals in cleaning products, a small group of Belgian scientists decided to find an environmentally-friendly way. Starting from a tiny shed, they developed a phosphate-free formula and launched Ecover. 'Eco' refers to ecology and 'ver' to the French word 'vert' (green). The product first appeared in supermarkets in Belgium ten years later. Ecover products began to be sold in the UK in 1991.

Electrolux Swedish company Elektrolux was formed in 1919, initially selling vacuum cleaners in various European countries; it entered the British market in 1928. The spelling of the company's name was changed to Electrolux in 1957.

Epson is the English-language acronym for 'Son of Electronic Printer' coined by Seiko Epson Corporation, which had started during the second world war as a maker of watch components. This miniature technology was spun off into precision parts needed to time the 1964 Tokyo Olympics and print the statistics, following which a consumer printer was developed, first dot-matrix and subsequently inkjet. Forays into personal computing proved unsuccessful and were abandoned in favour of cameras and scanning equipment.

Esso derives from a New York-centred subsidiary of one of the 34 companies formed in 1911 when Standard Oil was broken up to comply with US anti-trust law. In 1934 this name was applied to Standard Oil's first British subsidiary and retained it long after Standard Oil of New Jersey was rebranded ExxonMobil in 1971. In this way it has sidestepped being tarnished with reminders of the ecological disaster off Alaska in 1989.

Expedia was founded in 1996 as a division of Microsoft and was originally going to be called Microsoft Travel. However this idea was dropped before trading began and the made-up name Expedia, to suggest exploration and speed, was adopted. Microsoft completed sale of the company to InterActiveCorporation (IAC) in 2003 and they own it today with many new subsidiaries either set up or acquired since.

The Esso oil drop man appeared in the company's advertising for a few years from 1958 until superseded by the Tiger in your Tank campaigns.

Facebook began in 2004 as Harvard student Mark Zuckerberg's crass attempt to expand the pictorial directories used by American colleges (face books) to build a database to rate his campus's best-looking girls, for which he was almost expelled. Rapidly expanding beyond the Ivy League to most US colleges and funded extensively by interested venture capitalists, Facebook opened to everyone in 2005 and began making a profit in 2009; by 2012 it had reached the milestone of a billion users.

Fairy Liquid was launched in the UK in 1950 as one of the early liquid washing-up detergents. Blocks of green Fairy Soap (now discontinued) dated back to the 1830s and the Fairy name was literally a household one when the liquid detergent was introduced by the same company in soft plastic bottles that made it easy to squeeze out the required amount of liquid.

Fanta was established in World War 2 as the German arm of Coca-Cola's answer to having been cut off from its markets by the declaration of war; using only leftover apple fibre and whey from the manufacturing process, head of production Max Keith urged his employees to use their imagination (Fantasie) in dreaming up a name for the resulting successful drink. Post-war, Coca-Cola resumed ownership of what production fell within West Germany and relaunched Fanta using Italian oranges. Since then, over ninety Fanta flavours have been created.

FedEx is the commonly used contraction of Memphis-based shipping company Federal Express, which was so widespread in use that it was formally adopted in 2000 and now adorns vehicles and publicity in characteristic purple and orange. Having acquired competitor TNT, FedEx's chief rival in the modern era is UPS (United Parcel Service).

Ferrero Rocher Pietro Ferrero began making his own chocolate in 1942 in his home town of Alba in Italy, beginning industrial scale production in 1946. His chocolates were first sold outside Italy in 1956 and were introduced in the UK in 1966. Now best known in this country for Ferrero Rocher chocolates, these luxury items were created and introduced in 1982 by his son and successor in the business Michele, who named them after a grotto in the Roman Catholic shrine of Lourdes, Rocher de Massabielle. Rocher is a French word and means rock.

Fiat is the Italian initials of *Fabbrica Italiana Automobili Torino*, producers of jaunty and eminently likeable cars in Turin since 1899. Owned for most of its history by the Agnelli family, the company has had its ups and downs, with exports to the USA tailing off after bright beginnings but establishing solid outposts in Latin America and even selling licences to Poland and the Soviet Union.

Ford Henry Ford built his first experimental car in a workshop behind his home in Detroit in 1896. After formation of the Ford Motor Company, the first Ford car was assembled at a specially built plant in July 1903 and the first Ford cars were imported to Britain the same year. Five years later, in 1908, the highly successful Model T was introduced. Mass produced, it was a car that famously his customers could have in any colour they liked so long as it was black. Production began in Britain in 1911.

Formica was first sold in 1912 and is a heat-resistant, wipe-clean laminate of paper or textile with melamine resin so called because the new product acted as a substitute for mica, a naturally occurring mineral dust. The word already existed as the scientific name for wood ants, from which formic acid and the derivative formaldehyde compound used in the resin were first isolated.

Fortnum & Mason was an unlikely combination of Queen
Anne's footman (William Fortnum) and his landlord (Hugh
Mason); together they sold at a profit the unused candle
wax from the household of Queen Anne. With that income,
they established a grocery on Piccadilly in 1707 and
future generations of Fortnums continued royal patronage,
upgrading the quality of foodstuffs accordingly, though two
claimed innovations (the baked bean and the Scotch egg) are
not quite so upmarket now. Since 1856, when Queen Victoria
was on the throne, the company has provided grocery items to
the monarch.

Opposite: Fry's Heinz
advert from 1878.

Foster's Irish-American brothers William and Ralph Foster,
immigrants to Australia, began brewing Foster's Lager in
Melbourne in November 1888. It was made available to the
Australian public from February 1889. It was not until 1971 that
the beer was imported into England. The European rights to the
beer are now owned by Heineken International.

Fray Bentos This name is derived from the port of Fray Bentos
in Uruguay where the company's products were originally
processed and packaged until the 1960s. Cattle farming and meat
processing have long been the main industries in Uruguay and
Fray Bentos products go back to 1863. The company's famous
tinned steak and kidney pie was introduced in 1961.

Fry's chocolate Like Joseph Rowntree and the Cadbury
Brothers, Joseph S Fry, who founded Fry's chocolate in 1822,
was a Quaker. A patent for the manufacture of chocolate was
first granted to Walter Churchman in 1729. In 1756 Joseph Fry, a
pharmacist, began to sell chocolate from his apothecary in Bristol
and in 1761, on the death of the chocolate pioneer Churchman's
son, he took over their business. Fry's Chocolate Cream was first
sold in 1866 and is the only product to be sold under the Fry's
name today. In 1919 Fry's was taken over by Cadbury's, which in
turn was taken over by the American company Kraft Foods (now
named Mondelez) in 2011.

Gale's A.W. Gale of Marlborough was one of three large-scale
beekeepers in England and introduced his brand of honey to the
market in 1919.

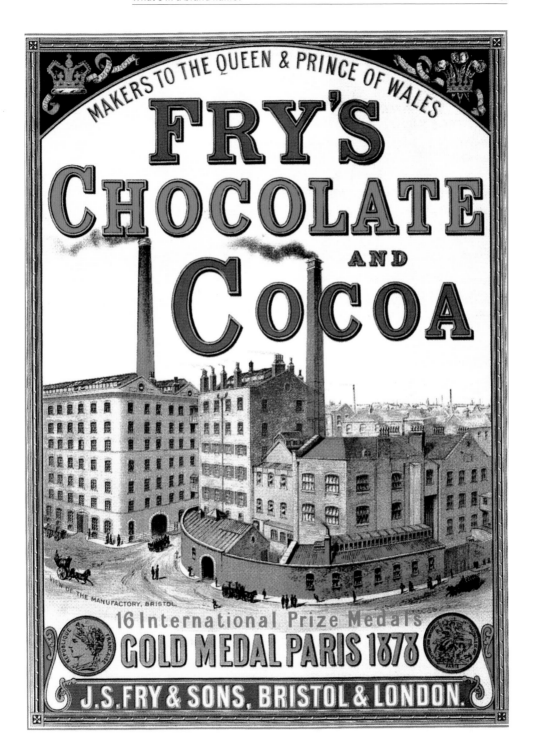

Garnier is a brand of the French cosmetics company L'Oréal for hair care and skin care products. The brand name comes from Frenchman Alfred Garnier, who set up Laboratoires Garnier in 1904 to produce his patented plant-based hair lotion. The Garnier company was acquired by L'Oréal in the 1970s and is today its second-largest brand.

Opposite: An advert for Gillette razors from 1924.

George is a brand of clothes sold by Asda in the UK and parent Walmart in the US. It was named by George Davies, who moved from Next to Asda in 1995 to create the label.

Giffgaff is said to be an old Scottish word meaning 'mutual giving'. It was chosen to fit with the principles of the company, with a bow also to founder Gav Thompson's first name. The strapline for Giffgaff is 'the mobile network run by you' to reflect the fact that some users of the service help run various aspects of the operation.

Gillette takes its name from America businessman King C Gillette, who founded a company to produce safety razors in 1901. His invention later spread to other countries worldwide. From the early 1930s until recently an impressive Art Deco building on London's Great West Road was the company's European HQ.

Ginsters is a relative latecomer to snack foods, starting only in 1969 after the eldest son of the Ginster family wound up ventures in horse manure and clotted cream in favour of building a factory to produce Cornish pasties in their home region. The products, later joined by pork pies and associated baked savouries, gained maximum exposure through their sale to petrol stations and successful positioning as cheap, no-nonsense snacks.

Google One of the world's biggest technology companies may have started with a typo. Co-founder Larry Page was at a brainstorming session for a new and massive data indexing website. Someone suggested 'googolplex' — one of the largest describable numbers. Page shortened it to 'googol.' But it is said that when he later checked for the availability of the domain name, he made a mistake and typed in google instead. He liked the name and registered it.

By appointment
to His Royal
Highness The
Prince of Wales

"I'm no novice at shaving,

So take my tip."

" As I run my fingers over my face after the shave I realise more than ever what the Gillette Shaving Service means to me.

Smoothness everywhere! Comfort all the time! No bother with strops and hones! Shaving that is a delightful treat instead of an irksome task!"

That is the Gillette Service—available for every man with a beard to shave.

Write for Illustrated Booklet.

Gillette Safety Razor, Ltd.,
184-188 Great Portland St., London, W.1.

NEW IMPROVED GILLETTE
STANDARD SET .. 21/-
Other Gillette outfits 21/- and
upwards, down to 5/-
Obtainable at Stores, Cutlers, Iron-mongers, Hairdressers, Chemists and Jewellers.

Use the Gillette Safety Razor

TRADE Gillette MARK

KNOWN THE WORLD OVER

NO STROPPING NO HONING

"The shave with the smile in it"

Green & Black's was founded in 1991 by the couple Craig
Sams and Josephine Fairley, organic food pioneer and journalist
respectively. 'Green' stood for the environmental concerns of
the founders and 'Black' for the high cocoa solids chocolate they
wished to provide. In May 2005 Green & Black's was bought by
Cadbury. Today it is part of the Mondelez empire.

Green Giant In 1903 a small canned vegetable company was
born in the United States with the name Minnesota Valley
Canning Company. The Green Giant made his first appearance
in 1925. He was named after a particularly large variety of pea
harvested and sold by the company. In 1950 he became the
symbol for the company when the Minnesota Valley Company
became the Green Giant Company. The brand arrived in the UK
in 1960.

Greggs grew out of John Gregg's employment as a baker; in
1951 he opened his first shop in Newcastle. Under his two sons,
expansion began with amassing the assets of bakers up and
down the country. The big push to rebrand them all as Greggs
was occasioned by the purchase of The Bakers Oven, a more
significant competitor with over a hundred branches.

Gucci is the surname, and most of the Christian name, of
founder Guccio Gucci, but its quintessentially Italian image has
surprisingly British roots, as Gucci, working at the Savoy as a
teenager, observed the luggage being toted by guests in pre-first
world war London and took the inspiration back to Florence,
where he opened a leather goods shop that quickly established a
reputation for quality that has been sustained though the years,
even though ownership has since passed out of the hands of the
Gucci family.

Guinness was first brewed in 1759 in Dublin, after Arthur
Guinness took a 9,000-year(!) lease on St James's Brewery,
though the company has been headquartered in London in 1932.
The drink itself was one of just three variants of porter brewed,
the signature dark colour deriving from roasting a proportion
of the barley used, whilst the creamy head is from mixing the
beer with nitrogen and carbon dioxide. Guinness and Grand
Metropolitan were merged in 1997 to form Diageo.

Opposite: one of a long
series of memorable
Guinness adverts, this
example from 1934.

H&M This clothing retailer got its start in Sweden. In 1947, 30-year-old Erling Persson launched a women's clothing retailer called Hennes, the Swedish word for 'hers', in Västerås, Sweden. The company grew in popularity throughout Scandinavia and in 1968 Persson acquired another, very different company called Mauritz Widforss. Mauritz was a hunting and fishing retailer but Persson decided to have the merged companies stick to clothing, though he did expand his offerings to men's and children's clothing as well. He changed its name to Hennes & Mauritz and H&M as we know it today was born.

Haagen-Dazs Entrepreneur Reuben Mattus invented the vaguely Danish-sounding name for the premium ice cream brand in the 1960s. He founded the company in the Bronx, and thought the name Haagen-Dazs conveyed an "aura of old-world traditions and craftsmanship".

Halfords is today best associated with bicycles, but before their widespread adoption Frederick Rushbrooke had set himself up as the proprietor of an ironmongery in Birmingham. In 1892 he took premises on Halford Street in Leicester and began selling bike parts. Automotive accessories and sundry car parts followed over the years, eventually including audio, whilst the company spent time owned by Burmah Oil before passing into the hands of the Boots Group and then CVG.

Haribo is a German confectionery company founded in Bonn by Hans Riegel Sr. The name, registered in Germany in 1920, is formed by the first two letters in each of the names Hans Riegel Bonn. Haribo sweets were introduced in the UK in 1994. Today they sell worldwide and each language has its own company rhyme, the English variant being "Kids and grown-ups love it so, the happy world of Haribo!".

Hartley's Jam began in 1871 when William Pickles Hartley, a Lancashire greengrocer, had a consignment of jam go missing. Instead of letting his customers down he decided to make his own jam to sell in earthenware pots. Following the abolition of sugar duty in 1874, Hartley sold the grocery business and established a small jam factory in Bootle, Lancashire. Distribution grew to cover the North and the Midlands, and then in 1901 a factory was opened in Bermondsey, the centre for the fruit preserving trade, in order to cater for the London market. William P. Hartley Ltd was one of the largest canning and preserves companies in Britain when it was acquired by Schweppes in 1959.

Heineken On 15 February 1864, a young man named Gerard Adriaan Heineken (1841–1893) convinced his wealthy mother to buy De Hooiberg (The Haystack) brewery in Amsterdam, a popular working-class brand founded in 1592. In 1873 Heineken hired a student of Louis Pasteur to develop a yeast and the first Heineken brand beer was brewed. The company's lager was introduced in the UK in the 1950s, but lager beers did not become popular in this country until the 1970s.

Heinz The H. J. Heinz foods company was founded in 1869 in Pennsylvania by Henry John Heinz. The company's first product was horseradish. According to the brand's website, Henry was travelling on a train in New York in 1896 when a sign advertising '21 styles of shows' caught his eye and gave him the idea of using a number for his company's wide variety of products. At the time, Heinz was manufacturing more than 60 products – but Henry chose his lucky number 57 instead. This has been used in association with the Heinz brand for over 100 years, though there have always been over 57 varieties of the company's products during this period.

1950s Heinz advert.

IT'S GOOD - IT'S QUICK - IT'S
HEINZ

Hellmann's got its start when a German immigrant to America, Richard Hellmann, and his wife Margaret opened a delicatessen in New York in 1913. He created his own recipe of mayonnaise in the 1920s and this was perfected by his wife. Its fame then spread to many parts of the world.

His Master's Voice (HMV) Artist Francis Barraud noticed how his Jack Russell Terrier 'Nipper' often curiously examined the phonograph (the cylinder record player) that they had at home. Barraud named the painting 'Dog looking at and listening to a Phonograph', and eventually he decided to rename his work 'His Master's Voice.' At one point, he tried his luck exhibiting it at the Royal Academy, but without success. Advertising companies and clients were not impressed either, saying that no-one would know what the dog was doing. On 31st May 1899 Barraud went to borrow a brass horn, to replace the black one on the painting, from the Maiden Lane offices of The Gramophone Company. A manager of the company, Barry Owen, decided to buy the painting. It then became a highly successful trademark and the Company registered it as a trademark in July 1900. In recent times HMV has struggled to survive and is currently owned by a Canadian company who bought it from company administrators in 2019. Today, the 'His Master's Voice' trademark is used only as a marketing brand for surviving HMV shops.

Holland & Barrett was originally a grocery in Bishop's Stortford opened in 1870 by Major William Holland and Alfred Slapps Barrett. Vitamins and supplements have become the company's major selling point in recent years, with the stores branded in a uniform dark green.

Hoover is the generic term for a vacuum cleaner, to the extent that the competition's devices are also customarily referred to as 'hoovers'. Invented in 1908 by Canton, Ohio janitor James Murray Spangler, his Electric Suction Sweeper incorporated a filter by Bissell (themselves still a popular name in the field). Spangler's cousin's husband William Henry Hoover bought the patent and set to manufacturing the devices, which by the 1930s took their familiar form with a shell of Bakelite (a light but tough plastic invented by Begian Leo Baekeland) covering the exposed pipework. Hoover also made washing machines, ultimately attracting the attention of Maytag, which bought the company from the Hoover family in 1986.

Hotpoint In 1903, Earl Richardson, a meter reader and plant superintendent for an electric power company in Ontario, California, developed a small, lightweight version of the heavy, cumbersome electric iron first patented in 1882. Richardson's invention was eventually named Hotpoint, after the heating elements that converged in the iron's tip, allowing it to be used to press around buttonholes and in and around ruffles and pleats on clothing and curtains. Meanwhile, 33-year old George Hughes from Iowa was designing the first electric range cooker. In 1918, Richardson and Hughes joined forces, merging their companies with the General Electric Company and creating the Hotpoint brand of appliances.

House of Fraser was founded by the partnership of Glasgow drapers Hugh Fraser and James Arthur in 1849, first under the name Arthur and Fraser. The dissolution of the partnership in 1865 brought the retail arm under Fraser and several subsequent generations of the family expanded the business, acquiring department store competitors and land at favourable lease conditions. More recently the firm has been owned by the Al Fayed family, but struggles in the past decade have delivered it into the hands of Mike Ashley's Sports Direct.

Hovis In 1886 a man named Richard 'Stoney' Smith, a baker from Stone in Staffordshire, changed the way that flour was milled. He perfected a method of steam cooking that preserved wheatgerm in bread without destroying its nutrients. For generations, the wheatgerm had been discarded with the bran when making white flour. Stoney's genius was to steam it before adding it to wholemeal flour, producing a new kind of bread with three times the natural germ but without the grittiness that was associated with other wholemeal breads at the time. A national competition with a prize of £25 was launched in 1890 to find a name for this new wheatgerm bread. Herbert Grime came up with the winning name Hovis, short for *hominis vis* (strength of man, Latin). Associated thereafter with northern robustness, Hovis ran a much-loved television advert during the 1970s in which a boy with a northern accent wrestled his bicycle up a steep and picturesque hill – in Shaftesbury, Dorset.

HP Sauce extols the Houses of Parliament, which had begun serving Nottingham grocer Frederick Gibson Garton's tomato-based brown sauce in its restaurant concessions in 1895. Heinz, upon its takeover of the company in 2005, controversially closed the Aston factory and relocated production to the Netherlands.

HSBC, or Hongkong and Shanghai Bank, is a British banking giant despite its name, and is best known in the modern era for acquiring and subsuming the Midland Bank in 1992. This major change was accompanied by the transfer of headquarters to London from Hong Kong, prior to the latter's handover to China in 1997.

Hush Puppies An American shoe company sales manager sat with a friend for a dinner of catfish and deep fried corn fritters called 'hush puppies.' Intrigued by the name, the salesman discovered that farmers also used these hush puppies to quiet barking dogs. In the US at that time, tired feet were known as 'barking dogs' and the salesman reasoned that his soft, lightweight shoes could 'quiet' feet too. The shoes, with this name having been adopted, were first shown at a shoe fair in Chicago in 1957. Prince Philip chose Hush Puppies to wear on a 1959 visit to the United States at the same time celebrities like Warren Beatty, Frank Sinatra, Dean Martin and Perry Como were also wearing them. It was reported that Hush Puppies' rubber soles saved the life of Rolling Stones guitarist Keith Richards when he accidentally touched his guitar against an ungrounded microphone at a 1965 concert in Sacramento, California.

Hush Puppies advert, 1968.

IKEA stands for *Ingvar Kamprad Elmtaryd Agunnaryd*, the last two words being the name of the farm in Sweden the founder grew up on and its associated village. The house colours of blue and yellow similarly evoke the Swedish flag, and the company's competitively-priced wooden furniture products all have Swedish words as names, no matter the territory in which they are sold. The company says that the correct pronunciation is 'Ee-kay-ah' rather than the usual English pronunciation 'Eye-key-ah'.

Imperial Leather In the 1930s, Cussons (named after founder
Thomas Cussons) launched Imperial Leather soap, based on an
original 'Eau de Cologne Imperiale Russe' fragrance from 1798.
'Leather' successfully conveyed the air of luxury the company
wanted to associate with the soap. Cussons was one of the first
soap companies to invest in radio programme sponsorship
in America, especially for popular drama serials. It was this
investment that led to the use of the phrase 'soap operas' in
relation to such shows, a term later transferred to television both
there and here in the UK.

Indesit was founded in Italy in 1953 with the name Spirea and its
first products were coolers. In 1956 the company name changed
twice: first to Indel (*Industria Elettrodomestici*) and then to
Indes (*Industria Elettrodomestici SpA*). Another Italian company
Merloni Elettrodomestici (founded 1975) bought Indesit in 1987.
The firm then became *Industria Elettrodomestici Spirea Italia
SpA*. Indesit UK has been based in Peterborough since 2003.

Irn-Bru is a phonetic Glaswegian rendering of Iron Brew,
a trademark from which Barr's, the brewers of this orange-
coloured sugary drink since 1901, needed to distance themselves
when production was resumed after the war in 1946. Proposed
branding laws forced them to alter the name as the drink is not
actually brewed. Irn-Bru also contains no iron, despite cheeky
advertising that claims it's made from girders.

Itsu in Japanese means 'whenever'. Founder Julian Metcalfe
wanted to give people the opportunity of good but affordable
Japanese cuisine at any time of day. The idea for what became
a chain came from a visit to Japan in 1994, when he noted that
every bento box was a work of art. The first Itsu opened in
Chelsea in 1997, followed in 2000 by one in Soho. Over 75 more
have opened since.

Jaeger was established in 1884 by British businessman Lewis
Tomalin as 'Dr Jaeger's Sanitary Woollen System Co Ltd' to
capitalise on a craze for wool-jersey long johns inspired by the
theories of German scientist Dr Gustav Jaeger, who promoted the
benefits of animal hair in clothing. By the early part of the 20th
Century the Jaeger brand was associated with high fashion.

John Lewis opened a drapery on Oxford Street in 1864, but it was his son, also named John, who developed the John Lewis Partnership by which all branches are held in a trust and profits shared. Progress thereafter brought in Waitrose, Peter Jones and early iterations of Selfridge's, all resolutely upmarket. Even with today's coronavirus-related difficulties, there remain over fifty stores operating, and the company's latter-day Christmas TV adverts have become much cherished.

Johnson & Johnson ought really to have been founded as Johnson, Johnson & Johnson, as these were three American brothers from New Jersey who in 1886 began manufacturing surgical dressings. Expansion into commercial drug research by the 1930s was assisted by direct marketing of the products developed by the laboratories and, later still, medical equipment was produced. Today's ventures include biotechnology and vaccine research. The familiar logo derives from the signature of founder James Wood Johnson.

Kellogg's cornflakes came about quite by accident when the wheat being rolled by W.K. and Dr. John Harvey Kellogg at the Battle Creek Sanitarium in Michigan during 1894 came out as flat flakes rather than the intended granola. These were wildly popular and spawned multiple ranges, establishing the consumption of toasted cereal as an American breakfast ritual that spread worldwide. This is another signature-based logo, tweaked only subtly over the years but still evoking that of W. K. Kellogg.

Kenco is the abbreviation (from 1962) of the Kenya Coffee Company, founded in London in 1923 to sell the same to country houses by mail order. The modern name has accordingly drifted from its roots to reflect the fact that the sale of espresso machines subsequently became a major part of the business.

Kenwood The name Kenwood refers to founder Kenneth Wood, who in 1947 set up a business, the Kenwood Manufacturing Company, in his garage in Woking, Surrey. The first Kenwood product was the A100 toaster, but in 1950 he invented the Kenwood Chef food mixer, which found a market all over the world.

Kia is a Korean word translated as 'to rise from Asia'. The company has roots from 1944, when it was started as the Kyungsung Precision Industry. It started by manufacturing steel tubing and bicycle parts. Its first bicycle, known as the Sumchully, was manufactured in Korea in 1951. Then, a year later, they changed the company name to Kia Industries. The company built small motorcycles from 1957, trucks from 1962 and cars from 1974. Kia started trading in the UK in 1991, selling just under 1,800 cars in its first year.

Kingsmill was named after William King, the founder of a flour mill in Uxbridge where the original Kings mill was built in 1836. Today the company is owned by Allied Bakeries.

KitKat was a term for mutton pies served at the London gentlemen's club of the same name during the nineteenth century. Rowntree's trademarked the name (in multiple spellings) and in 1937 applied it to a four-finger chocolate bar the company created two years earlier. A billion KitKats are produced every year, including the KitKat Chunky, which consists of just one huge finger. The brand is today owned by Nestlé. Hershey produce KitKats under licence in the USA.

An early version of the KitKat bar.

Kleenex tissues were introduced by Kimberly-Clark in the US in 1924 as a cold cream and make-up remover, and were launched in the UK the following year. They had their origin in paper filters produced by the company for gas masks in the first world war. The need for a new name for the tissues based on the word 'clean' and that could be registered as a trade mark led to 'Kleenex'. In 1929 Kimberly-Clark's head researcher was suffering from hay fever and started using the tissues in place of his handkerchief. The idea took off and sales doubled in the first year of their being promoted as paper handkerchiefs.

Knight's Castile soap was introduced by John Knight Ltd in 1919. Castile is a name that refers generally to olive oil based soap made in a style similar to that originating in the Castile region of Spain. Today the soap brand is part of Unilever.

Kobo is an ebook seller and the name is simply an anagram of book. It originated as Shortcovers, a cloud e-reading service launched by the Canadian bookstore chain Indigo Books and Music in February 2009. In December 2009, Indigo renamed the service Kobo and spun it off into an independent company.

Kodak was perhaps the first trademark deliberately designed to be distinctive; already fond of the letter K, George Eastman thus bookended the new word in 1888, when his company was formed, to underscore its perceived uniqueness and impossibility of mispronunciation whatever the local language. A century of solid dominance in the film photography arena followed but was brought rudely to a halt when the company missed the boat on digital, and since bankruptcy in 2012 what remains has shifted to the field of medical research and development.

KP Nuts takes its initials from Kenyon Produce, a later name for Kenyon & Son started by Charles Kenyon in 1853. From its beginnings trading in various foods, principally pickles, the company turned its hand to crisps in the 1940s. KP launched its first packaged nuts in 1952 with Roasted Salted Hazelnuts and the first Roasted Salted Peanuts followed in 1953.

Kraft was the surname of Chicago door-to-door wholesale cheese salesman James L. Kraft. Bolstered by the development of pasteurisation, which attracted major sales of the resulting long-lasting processed cheese to the US Army during the first world war, Kraft's company was just one of several to come under the aegis of the National Dairy Products Corporation, but the name was re-used in 1969 to rebrand the entire organisation.

Kronenbourg 1664 sounds as German as it's possible to be, but derives from a village in the Alsace region of France, which traditionally spoke a Germanic dialect, and has thus pinged back and forth over the years between France and a covetous Germany. In the titular year, Geronimus Hatt brewed a golden pale lager with local Strisselpalt hops, and this was remembered when the brewery made a big push post-war to sell its lager to Britain. It is now produced under licence by Heineken.

Lacoste was the brainchild of French tennis champion René Lacoste, and its signature crocodile logo evoked how he dealt with opponents on the court. His eponymous tennis shirts, in partnership with knitwear magnate André Gillier, have remained at the forefront of the sport since 1933.

Lancôme This beauty product company, founded in 1935, was named after the ruins of a castle, Le Château de Lancosme, that founder Armand Petitjean visited while on vacation in the French countryside. His inspiration for the company symbol, a rose, was the many wild roses growing around the castle. The company began with a range of five perfumes.

Lavazza is an Italian manufacturer of coffee products founded in Turin in 1895 by Luigi Lavazza. It was initially run from a small grocery store in the city. Lavazza Coffees Ltd was established in London in 1990 to bring the brand to Britain.

Lego This Danish company, set up in 1932, used two Danish words, *leg* and *gotd*, which mean 'play well' to arrive at its name. It made stepladders, ironing boards, stools and wooden toys and the name Lego was used from 1934. The company's most famous product, interlocking blocks of plastic, was introduced in 1949 with the name Automatic Binding Bricks. Initially this was sold only in Denmark. From 1953 the company's name was stamped on each block and the name has been associated with this toy construction product ever since. As part of the company's expansion, British Lego Ltd was established in 1959.

Lenovo was known as 'Legend' for 15 years before receiving its current name in 2003. It was under this new name that Lenovo would have its first successes outside its home country, China, where it was well known as a brand leader. At the end of 2004, Lenovo bought IBM's personal computer division giving it a major foothold in the West. Keeping the first two letters of its previous name, Lenovo changed the second part to a Latin word for new.

Levi's are the denim jeans manufactured by Levi Strauss, a Bavarian immigrant to San Francisco whose riveted work clothes, first made in 1849, proved especially hard-wearing. The development of the company's signature 501 jeans in 1890 was followed in subsequent decades by their adoption by multiple youth subcultures, even if tastes for this fashion have tailed off in recent years.

LG was previously called Lucky Goldstar, which was formed from two company names. Lak-Hui was a Korean chemical company formed in 1947 which later merged with a plastics and electronics company called GoldStar. As Lak-Hui is pronounced 'lucky', Lucky-Goldstar was the result. The company moved into producing televisions in 1966 and, later, into home computers and the name was changed to LG.

Libby's was founded in 1869 as Libby, McNeill & Libby in Chicago by Archibald McNeill and the brothers Arthur and Charles Libby. The business began with a canned meat product, beef in brine, or corned beef and today offers a wide range of processed foods.

Lidl was founded in Germany as a grocery wholesaler in the 1930s by Joseph Schwarz. He did not want to use his own name because Schwarz Markt would translate as 'black market' so he used the surname of a former business partner, A. Lidl, instead. The first Lidl stores were opened in Germany in 1973 and four years later there were 33 Lidl stores there. During the 1990s Lidl supermarkets started to open around the rest of Europe and today Lidl stores can be found in nearly every country in Europe. The first Lidl supermarkets in the UK opened in 1994 when a large distribution centre began operations in Lutterworth. There are now over 800 Lidl stores in the UK.

Lindt Swiss chocolatier Rodolphe Lindt was very successful when he introduced his chocolate fondant in 1879 but his factory in Bern was much too small. He could not cope with demand. But all that didn't bother him: He enjoyed his life and only went to the factory when he felt like it. Despite this he accepted an offer from the confectioner Jean Tobler for him to ensure even fuller order books for Lindt as a travelling salesman. In the mid-1890s, his small factory was ready for demolition; modernisation was vital. And there was the pressing question of how to reduce the pile of orders. It was then that he met a man, Johann Rudolf Sprungli-Shifferli, who had travelled especially from Zurich to meet him. Lindt sold the business to that man, who built a new factory near Zurich to cope with demand.

Lipton began as a grocery run by the parents of Glaswegian Thomas Lipton (1848-1931), who had encountered tea on his travels as a youth and invested heavily in the crop through bypassing established supply chains worldwide. The tea arm, distinct from the cafés, gradually came into the hands of Unilever and today is partially owned by PepsiCo.

Lloyds Bank began as Taylors & Lloyds in Birmingham in 1765 and for the first hundred years the Bank operated from just one office in the town. The name came from John Taylor, Sampson Lloyd and their two sons who founded the bank. The Lloyd family were Quakers and were actively involved in the movement to abolish the transatlantic slave trade. From the 1860s Lloyds Bank embarked on a period of rapid expansion and growth.

Londis is short for London District Stores and was established in 1959 by a group of London independent retail grocers who had the aim of establishing a fully operational wholesale company owned jointly by the retailers it served. Since then it has developed into a nationwide chain of convenience stores. It was bought by the Booker Group, owners of Tesco, in 2017.

Early 1950s Lucozade magazine advert.

Lucozade began life as Glucozade. It is made predominantly from a mixture of Glucose syrup and carbonated water and was first developed in 1927 by a Newcastle chemist William Owen for his son who was recovering from jaundice. The name changed to Lucozade in 1929 when it began to enter a wider market as a drink to assist people in recovering energy after illness. It is now more associated as a sports drink following its promotion as such from the late 1980s.

Lurpak was set up in 1901 as a combination of several Danish dairy farmers to create a common brand for butter to increase sales. The distinctive logo is based on the 'Lur', an ancient musical instrument once used in Denmark.

Lyons Maid ice-creams and lollies, created in 1925, were products of the J. Lyons & Co firm of tea shops, helping propel the company's diversification into food products. The dancing children logo identified the brand in sweet shops and lasted until Nestlé purchased it in 1992. Revival came in 2008 when subsequent owner Froneri reintroduced the Lyons Maid brand to capitalise on nostalgia.

Lyons Tea The first Lyons tea shop was opened by the J. Lyons family in September 1894 at 213 Piccadilly. Tea, coffee, bread, cakes and pies, which had originally been produced for the tea rooms, began to be sold directly to the customer from 1902. The tearooms and corner houses fell out of favour with the public and the last one closed in 1976. Lyons tea, cakes, biscuits and ground coffee are still sold, but without the presence they once had.

Maytag The Maytag Washing Machine Company was founded in 1893 by Frederick Maytag. The company later branched out to make other kitchen appliances but washing machines remain one of its main products.

M&Ms are likened to Smarties by Britons, and indeed spring from when Mars Company scion Forrest S. Mars Junior noticed Spanish Civil War fighters eating the hard-shelled (and thus non-melting) British chocolates and copied them. One of the Ms in the name is his own; the other of Bruce Murrie, an heir himself but of Hershey's Chocolates, which took a 20% share upon the commencement of production in 1981. The treats were little-known in Britain until the advent of *E.T.* (1982), in which they were a significant part of the plot and thus marketed heavily – a hugely successful and influential example of product placement that Hershey's had first employed in a motion picture back in 1927 with an Academy Award winning film titled *Wings*.

McCain The McCain brothers (Wallace, Harrison, Robert and Andrew) were sons of a third-generation farmer. They used their family knowledge of agriculture and combined it with innovation. The brothers opened the first McCain Foods production facility in 1957 in their home town of Florenceville, New Brunswick, Canada. Here they began producing the frozen chips for which they are best known.

McDonald's was the name of the restaurant opened in San Bernardino, California by brothers Dick and Mac McDonald in 1940. In spite of the global recognition enjoyed by the name ever since, the titular brothers found themselves muscled out of the company by Ray Kroc, the businessman they had engaged in 1955 to automate hamburger production. Ronald McDonald, the clown mascot employed from shortly thereafter until recently, is not a blood relation.

The first McDonald's.

McVitie's Robert McVitie, born in 1809, started his working life as an apprentice baker in Edinburgh, setting up on his own in 1830. In 1875 Charles Price joined the firm and helped to grow the brand, opening a new factory in the suburbs of that city in 1888. McVitie & Price's first major biscuit was the McVitie's Digestive, created in 1892 by a new young employee at the company named Alexander Grant. The biscuit was given its name because it was thought that its high baking soda content served as an aid to food digestion. Another big success for the company was its invention of the Jaffa Cake in 1927. By the time it introduced Hob-nobs in 1985, the company's name had shortened to McVitie's.

1950s advert for a long-established favourite.

Magners derives from the cider brewed in Clonmel since 1935 by William Magner. Two years later a 50% share was purchased by H.P. Bulmer, whose name adorned the company and its product upon the purchase in 1946 of the remaining share. Magners, however, was re-used to christen a stand-alone brand for sales outside the Republic of Ireland at the turn of the century, although both Bulmers and Magners are the same product.

Maltesers Despite the similarity in the name, Maltesers are not named after the people of Malta. The name is a portmanteau of the words 'malt' (one of the main ingredients) and 'teasers'. They were introduced by the Mars company in 1937, originally known as Energy Balls and marketed as slimming aids for women. This quintessentially British chocolate made it to the USA only in 2017.

Marabou is the word for a variety of African stork, a bird used as a logo by the original producers of the eponymous chocolate, production of which started in 1919. The brand is today owned by Mondelez.

Marks & Spencer had its beginnings in a Leeds market stall opened in 1884 by Michael Marks, an immigrant from Slonim in Russian Poland. Thomas Spencer was his first cashier, and from 1894, his business partner. Until the 1990s the company sold only British-made goods and established St Michael as the brand for its clothing. Although the company name is frequently abbreviated to M&S, a more irreverent name is Marks & Sparks which is acknowledged by the company through its Sparks loyalty card.

Marlboro is a cigarette name that derives from the Great Marlborough Street premises of the tobacconist established by Philip Morris, moved there from Bond Street by his widow in 1873. The Marlboro brand reached the USA in 1902 and became associated with Americana, ironically first marketed to women through the use of filters. Post-war, the brand was revitalised by a turn to advertising towards men, giving rise to the iconic cowboy-themed Marlboro Man advertising. In recent years, the healthy living-related social opprobrium against cigarettes has demanded the removal of advertising altogether.

Marmite In 1902 the Marmite Food Company was founded in Burton-on-Trent where the raw material, yeast, was readily available from the town's brewers. Marmite is the word for a French cooking pot with a distinctive pot-bellied shape, similar to the crockery pots in which Marmite (albeit with the English pronunciation) was sold until glass jars of similar shape were developed in the 1920s. Invented by German scientist Justus von Liebig, this famous yeast extract passed via Best Foods to Unilever and is now produced by the same company as Bovril. Perceived by a roughly equal proportion of the populace as being delicious or disgusting, Marmite has become a metaphor for something that polarises opinions in the same manner.

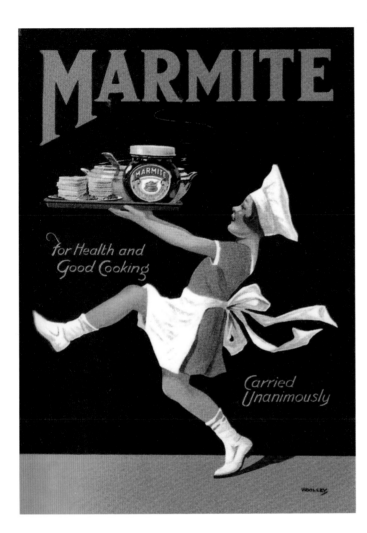

for Health and Good Cooking

Carried Unanimously

Early 20th century advert for Marmite.

Mars Franklin Clarence Mars, who began producing chocolate bars in America in 1923, started up in Britain when he leased a single room factory in Slough from May 1932. England was chosen for the company's European base because Mars could speak the language. He initially employed a staff of eight and, when introduced from August 1932, the Mars Bar was entirely handmade at first. The business prospered quickly and within a year two million Mars bars had been sold and 100 people were employed.

Matalan sounds exotically Spanish but actually combines the names of Matt and Alan, the two sons of founder John Hargreaves, who opened his first fashion and homewares shop in Bamber Bridge in 1985. Rapid expansion followed, plus floating on the Stock Exchange but subsequent de-listing shortly after; the Hargreaves family is still in control.

Max Factor Maksymilian Faktorowicz, a beautician from Eastern Europe, set up this cosmetics company in 1909, wisely deciding on a shortening of his name for the purposes of the brand. He emigrated to the USA in 1914 and his firm's products went on to become favourites of Hollywood film stars.

Maxwell House is a brand of coffee introduced in 1892 by wholesale grocer Joel Owsley Cheek, it was named in honour of the now-defunct Maxwell House Hotel in Nashville, Tennessee, which was its first major customer.

Maynard's Bassetts Charles Maynard and his brother Tom started manufacturing sweets in 1880 in their kitchen in Stamford Hill, London. Next door, Charles's wife, Sarah Ann, ran a sweet shop selling their products. In 1896 the brothers formed the Maynards sweet company. The Bassett half comes from a company founded in Sheffield by George Bassett in 1842. Perhaps the company's best-known sweets, the Liquorice Allsorts, are said to have been created by accident in 1899 when a sales rep tripped and spilled his various varieties of sweets in front of a client. In 1926 the mascot of Bassett's, Bertie Bassett, was created and Bertie continues to represent the brand today. In 2016, the brand was joined with Maynards to create Maynard's Bassetts.

McCain Foods was founded in 1957 by four Canadian brothers of that surname to sell frozen food products, quickly becoming profitable and thus expanding. UK operations began in 1968 and within twelve years the signature McCain Oven Chips were introduced; today this is just one product of what has become the largest manufacturer of frozen potato products in the world.

Meccano is believed to come from the phrase "Make and Know" though no definitive record seems to have survived. What is known is that the children's building toy began life in 1902 as Mechanics Made Easy, under which name it had little success. Its inventor Frank Hornby (who went on in 1938 to begin production of model railways) then registered the name Meccano in 1907 and the toy then went on to achieve much greater sales.

Mercedes-Benz's constituent names derive from disparate sources. Karl Benz, inventor of the internal combustion engine, combined his resources with designer Gottlieb Daimler to produce Daimler-Benz automobiles, and by the turn of the century Austrian *bon vivant* Emil Jellinek began selling them to well-heeled customers on the French Riviera. He named the resulting 1901 35hp model after his daughter, Mercedes, and its record-breaking performance spurred sales to the extent that the name was adopted for all Daimler-Benz cars.

MG stands for Morris Garages, but was developed by Charles Kimber in the 1920s as a signature marque distinguishing Morris Oxfords sold by William Morris's sales and service centre in Oxford. MG was then spun off as its own identity, remaining distinct even through the merger with Austin and British Leyland, and just some of its popular models were the Midget and MGB. In later years the MG badge adorned upper-level Mini Metros and Maestros, and today survives in Chinese ownership.

Microsoft, founded in 1975 by Bill Gates and Paul Allen, stands for 'micro-computer software', and over the years developed into the pre-eminent manufacturer of computer operating software (ultimately known as Windows) and later the desktop computers that ran it. Although quick to exploit the Internet after its appearance in the mid-1990s, the company missed the boat on mobile phones in the following decade and has had to claw its way back to parity with Apple ever since.

Miele is a German manufacturer of domestic appliances and commercial equipment. The company was founded in 1899 by Carl Miele and Reinhard Zinkann, and has always been a family-owned and run company. The company's first washing machine was produced in 1903 and its first vacuum cleaner in 1931.

MINI, now in all-upper case, is today BMW's division establ-ished to produce the modern version of Sir Alec Issigonis's small British car. Its illustrious predecessor, envisaged by BMC as a fuel-efficient answer to the Suez crisis that had cut off the oil-consuming nations from its producers, was in production between 1959 and 2000 with few changes in appearance other than the bonnet badge. Over five million were produced.

Opposite: The Mini was launched in 1959 as the Austin Seven, but rebranded Mini in 1962.

Mondelez is a made up word from words for 'world' and 'delicious' in Latin and several other Romance languages. It was coined by two Kraft Foods employees after the company held an in-house renaming contest that inspired about 1,700 entries. The new name was adopted in 2012.

Monsoon Peter Simon began selling clothes in London markets and went on to open a retail shop in Beauchamp Place, Knightsbridge, in 1973. Simon chose the name of Monsoon for his company, recalling his own birth during a monsoon in Sri Lanka. Around the world by the beginning of 2020 there were over 1400 shops trading as Monsoon or its spin-off Accessorize, but the company went into administration in June and on repurchase by Simon some closures were made.

Morrisons The company was founded in 1899 by William Morrison, who started the business as an egg and butter merchant in Rawson Market, Bradford, operating under the name of Wm Morrison Limited. His son Ken Morrison took over the company in 1952, aged 21. In 1958, Morrison opened his and Bradford's first self-service shop. Three years later he opened in the same city the company's first supermarket. The company opened its 100th store, in Nelson, Lancs, in 1999 and its first store in the South of England, at Erith in Kent the same year. Today it has around 500.

Mr Kipling The Mr Kipling brand name first appeared on cakes in 1967. The company says, "Mr Kipling exists in the hearts and minds of Manor Bakeries' employees and all cake lovers, but not as a real person". He was invented by the advertising agency J. Walter Thompson to introduce an air of home-made authenticity to what was effectively a factory bakery owned by a foods conglomerate, Premier Foods.

How luxurious can an Austin Seven get?

Most people are very nicely satisfied thank you with *any* Austin Seven. Others want the earth. The new Austin Super Seven has been designed for them. It's got everything any other Austin Seven's got—high m.p.h. (70), high m.p.g. (50), large space inside (for seating four adults), small-space outside (for parking in 11 feet). *And it's got much more. Here's what.*

INSIDE New duotone trim in subtly blending colour-choices. Sound insulation to hush the engine to a gentle purr. Fuller cushions for greater comfort: thick new carpets. New oval-shaped instrument panel, including both oil-pressure and water-temperature gauges. And many many more extras.

OUT New duotone palette of brilliant colours to choose from. Much more dashing fine-mesh grille. It's altogether a gayer, brighter car. Add up the list of improvements when you see the new model at your Austin dealer. Price: £405 plus £186.17.3 Purchase Tax and surcharge

GET INTO AN AUSTIN AND OUT OF THE ORDINARY

NEW AUSTIN SUPER SEVEN

THE AUSTIN MOTOR COMPANY LIMITED • LONGBRIDGE • BIRMINGHAM

By Appointment to
Her Majesty The Queen
Motor Car Manufacturers
The Austin Motor
Company Limited

Backed by BMC 12-month
warranty and BMC service

Müller, a dairy staple in its native Bavaria since 1896, was a comparative latecomer to the UK but soon became significant, aided by the entertaining nature of its product packaging; for instance, the Fruit Corner yogurt in which an integral quarter of the packaging contained jam to add at the consumer's leisure. The company also revitalised the moribund rice pudding dish by including sauce in the same manner.

Nando's takes its name from the first-born son of joint founder Fernando Duarte, a Mozambican who with South African Robert Brozin liked a Johannesburg peri-peri chicken takeaway called Chickenland so much that they bought it. Today there are over a thousand of these restaurants worldwide, including over 400 in the UK.

Nationwide was originally the Southern Co-operative Building Society, formed in 1884 by Charles Cooper who wanted the mortgage lender to operate on the same principles as a Co-operative grocery store. Its first mortgage was of £120 for a terraced house in Battersea which was paid off in 1894. Following a number of mergers with other building societies all across the UK a new name was needed. In 1970, following some adverse publicity on a BBC television news and current affairs programme called Nationwide, it defiantly chose this name for its rebrand and has thrived ever since, today having around 700 branches.

NatWest is one of those popular abbreviations that was ultimately adopted by the company itself. It abbreviates National Westminster Bank, which combined the resources of National Provincial Bank and Westminster Bank in 1968 to set it up as one of the 'Big Four' clearing banks.

Neff Carl Neff set up a stove and oven workshop at his German home in 1877 and this developed into a thriving business making commercial ovens for use in the catering industry. His first mass-produced appliance for the home was a coal burning stove first sold in 1914. In 1949 the company produced the first domestic double oven to be available in Europe and in 1954 the first microwave ovens outside the USA, where they had been invented in 1946.

Nescafé is a portmanteau of 'Nestlé' and 'café', but has Brazilian roots not immediately apparent to this Swiss-associated corporation. In 1930 the Brazilian government combined with Nestlé to create an outlet for its coffee harvest surplus, together giving birth to Nescafé in 1938. This powdered product was further improved when freeze-drying was developed in the mid-1960s, creating the familiar and convenient instant coffee.

Nespresso is formed from Nestlé and expresso. The company was formed in 1986 by Nestlé to manufacture expresso machines. Nespresso machines brew coffee from capsules for home or professional use.

Nestlé is today the largest food company in the world, taking its current name from Henri Nestlé, a Swiss confectioner of German birth whose factory was merged with the Anglo-Swiss Milk Company in 1905. Several major brands have been acquired and remain in use such as Crosse & Blackwell, Findus, Rowntree Mackintosh and Carnation, though the best-known product is its chocolate.

Netflix, or flicks (films/movies) from the net, began in 1997 as a DVD rental business; having eclipsed the previous store-centred video rental model in short order, the company then came up against streaming and nearly crippled itself by attempting to separate the physical DVD arm under the name Qwikster. Having called this strategy off just in time, the company let DVD subscriptions tail off of their own accord, expanding sufficiently to begin producing original content of its own, to be purchased on its proprietary subscription network as a rival to cable and satellite broadcasters.

next is the modern name (and spelling) of the clothing stores established in 1864 by Joseph Hepworth in Leeds. Ready-to-wear suits were Hepworth & Son's business for the next century before womenswear retailer Kendall & Sons was acquired in 1981 and the idea coined to revamp this particular brand in the direction of high fashion. The brand was almost too successful thereafter, rapid expansion having to be curbed and money recouped by selling the Salisburys and Zales jewellery brands.

Nike, the Greek goddess of victory, was the name chosen in 1971 to rebrand seven-year-old Blue Ribbon Sports, founded by medal-winning track athletes Bill Bowerman and Phil Knight to import Japanese athletic shoes into the USA, from which grew the footwear and fashion giant of today. The unforgettable logo cost just $35 to commission and the founders didn't even care for it at first!

Nikon In September 1946, a new compact camera was introduced and named 'Nikon' by the Nippon Kagaku Company in Japan. The new name originated from 'NIKKO', based on letters from the company name to which the letter 'n' was added because it was felt this would give a more masculine impression.

Nintendo is credited with multiple possible derivations, the most evocative of which is a Japanese phrase that translates as 'leave luck to heaven'. The company harks back to the production of hand-made Japanese playing cards by Kyoto resident Fusajiro Yamauchi from 1889. Post-second world war, the current generation of the family achieved greater penetration of their latest plastic-backed cards by licensing Disney characters, but both this and a line of toys proved dead ends until maintenance engineer Gunpei Yokoi fortuitously incorporated electronics into an extendable arm he made in his spare time. Video games consoles followed in 1972, with Donkey Kong of 1981 the breakout product that cemented Nintendo's spot in arcades. This technology moved into smaller units like the Game and Watch handheld series, the modular Game Boy, and today's Switch, while console development begat the Playstation and Wii.

Nissan is the abbreviation for Nihon Sangyo, or Japan Industries, and the name first adorned cars in 1934; the name Datsun was also used (reflecting DAT Motors). Pre-war, American equipment was imported to build the cars and post-war an arrangement was struck to build Austin cars under licence. From these patents, smaller cars were developed that found their market in the USA when the oil crisis of 1973 sank demand for that country's traditionally larger cars. A reputation for build quality and reliability saw Nissan simultaneously make great headway in the UK, where strikes were slowly finishing off the domestic automotive industry. The Datsun name was dropped in 1986.

Nivea is a German personal care brand specialising in body care. It was founded in 1882 and is today owned by the Hamburg-based company Beiersdorf Global AG. The name Nivea is from a Latin word meaning 'snow-white'.

Nutella was first sold in Italy in 1963 and in the UK in 1964. The 'ella' suffix gave a feminine or 'sweet' touch to the brand name, variously pronounced as nut-tell-uh, new-teh-ya or new-tell-uh.

O2 recalls the periodic table designation for oxygen, but the telecom company's name is more prosaic in its derivation; when spun off from BT Cellnet in 2002, the resulting company was named mmO2 plc and three years later took the name O2. The company also sponsors the O2 Arena in North Greenwich, known as the Millennium Dome during its year as an exhibition centre but since revitalised as a prime concert venue.

Ocado Jez Frampton, CEO of Interbrand and non-executive director of Ocado, claims the made-up name 'Ocado' is intended to evoke fresh fruit. Neil Taylor, an Interbrand consultant, stated that the name was a variant on the avocado fruit.

Odeon Cinemas The name Odeon had been used by cinemas in France and Italy in the 1920s, but Andre Deutsch made it his own in the UK when he began the Odeon cinema chain here in 1930, two years after the first 'talking picture'. His publicity team claimed Odeon stood for "Oscar Deutsch Entertains Our Nation". However, the word is ancient Greek in origin, meaning 'singing place'. It was used for buildings built for musical shows, poetry competitions, and the like.

Olay is the subtly altered new name, since 1999, of what was historically more familiar in the UK as Oil of Ulay. Its origins are in South Africa, where Durban chemist Graham Wulff created a moisturiser product based on lanolin but consciously left its origins enigmatic, attracting customers through its perceived rarity and quality. Prior to the harmonisation of the product name, each sales territory had its own name for the product, variously Oil of Ulay (UK and Ireland), Oil of Ulan (Australia) or Oil of Olaz (Europe).

Opel traces its roots to a sewing machine manufacturer founded by Adam Opel in Rüsselsheim am Main, Germany, in 1862. The company began manufacturing bicycles in 1886 and cars in 1899. Opel still has its headquarters in the town of its founding.

Opposite: Rarely used today as such, Oxo cubes were once popular as a children's drink.

Orangina In 1935 a Spanish pharmacist by the name of Dr Trigo presented his new orange drink Naranjina at a Marseille trade fair. One of the visitors to take a keen interest in it was Frenchman Leon Beton who bought the concept and recipe for Naranjina from Dr Trigoin. Later that same year he introduced the drink, with the new name Orangina, in his home country. Enjoyed by tourists to the country, it became available outside France from 1984.

Oreo is a well-known American dark chocolate sandwich biscuit (or cookie in the US) whose name has as many possible origins as the modern product has varieties. Nabisco's immediate predecessor introduced them in 1912 and still produces them, albeit now as a Mondelez subsidiary.

Ovaltine was developed in Bern, Switzerland, where it is still sold under its original name, Ovomaltine (from ovum, Latin for egg, and malt, which were originally its main ingredients). Ovomaltine was exported to Britain in 1909; a misspelling of the name on the trademark application led to the name being shortened to Ovaltine in English-speaking markets.

OXO stock cubes have a name that probably derives from the oxen which went into what was originally a liquid meat extract developed in 1866 by Liebig's Extract of Meat Company (LEMCO); in 1910 the product was transformed into a dried, individually wrapped cube format and thus brought within the reach of family budgets. Production continues today under Premier Foods. The Oxo Tower on London's South Bank retains its name from long-time use as a cold store for the company, but is now a mixed-use building including several upmarket flats.

P&O abbreviates the Peninsular and Oriental Steam Navigation Company, founded in 1837 to ship cargo between England and Portugal; the flag logo of today has elements of both the Portuguese and Spanish flags.

Paddy Power is unashamedly Irish, combining the resources of three bookmakers in 1988 and adapting the surname of one of them, David Power. Having expanded early into the online arena, the company is best known for its green livery and unusual markets, offering odds on everything from the US presidential elections to the winners of *Big Brother* or *Love Island*.

Opposite: Palmolive advert from the 1930s.

Palmolive soap was introduced in America in 1898 and its ingredients included palm and olive oils, which gave rise to the name. It became so popular that the company which introduced it, the B J Johnson Company, renamed itself after the soap. In 1928 the company went on to purchase Colgate to become Colgate-Palmolive.

Panasonic This brand name was created from 'pan' (all) and 'sonic' (sound) and was adopted for worldwide use in 2003. When formed in Japan in 1918 its name was Matsushita and its first products were electrical components. It moved into audio in 1931 with its first radio. Its move into hi-fi began in 1970 with a new direct-drive turntable.

Parlophone is an Anglicised form of *Parlophon*, a label introduced in Germany in 1896 and brought to Britain (with the 'e') in 1923. *Parle* (French for speak) and *phon* (Greek for sound) are the constituents of the name, the company wisely avoiding the German equivalent 'Sprechenklang'. In the UK, Parlophone was regarded as the poor relation in the EMI family until it signed The Beatles in 1962. Parlophone was purchased by Warner Brothers in 2013.

Penguin Books The publisher's founder Allen Lane had already decided that he wanted an animal logo for his revolutionary new publishing house, which would make inexpensive but high-quality paperbacks available to the mass market. It was 1935 and, according to company legend, Lane's secretary suggested 'Penguin' as a "dignified, but flippant" name for the new company. Edward Young, a 21-year-old office junior, was immediately despatched to London Zoo to sketch the bird in every possible pose for the rest of the day. In 2013 Penguin merged with Random House. It has become the largest book publishing group in the UK with almost 25% of the market.

The **OLIVE OIL** in **PALMOLIVE**

Beautifies **BECAUSE IT...**

CLEANSES

AND SOOTHES

. . . provides a threefold Beauty Treatment . . .

The rich abundant lather of PALMOLIVE, derived from the natural vegetable oils of the olive and the palm, is so soft and velvety that it cannot hurt the most delicate skin. Yet when it is massaged well into the skin, and rinsed with warm water, then cold, there is nothing better for beauty than its gentle deep-cleansing action. Beauty experts have always known this —and that's why no less than 20,000 of them have unanimously recommended soap and water washing with an *olive oil* soap —Palmolive—as the best possible way of keeping your skin in the fresh, natural bloom of health.

PALMOLIVE

3ᵈ
per tablet

Pentax In 1952 Japanese lens company Asahi Optical introduced its first camera, the Asahiflex, the first Japanese SLR using 35mm film. The name Pentax was originally a registered trademark of the East German Zeiss Ikon company and came from 'Pentaprism' and 'Contax' (a brand name that had been used by Zeiss). The trade mark was acquired by the Asahi Optical company in 1957, who then branded their cameras Asahi Pentax (later becoming plain Pentax).

Perrier In 1898, Dr Louis Perrier became the owner of a French spring, which would later take his name. Water from the spring had been sold in bottles in France and Britain since 1863. Today the company is owned by Nestlé.

Adverts from the 1950s for two popular brands, including the very successful 'Persil Washes Whiter' slogan.

Pepsi was first mixed in New Bern, North Carolina in 1893 by Caleb Bradham, who called it Brad's Drink for its first five years, after which his desire to push the perceived digestive benefits of the sugary vanilla concoction prompted a new name, Pepsi-Cola, the name coming from the Greek pepsis, for digestion. Although the company went bust in 1923, it was bought by Loft Inc. and used to replace Coca-Cola in its soda fountains. Bottling from the 1930s brought sales to parity with Coca-Cola and established the long rivalry between the two companies. The logo, changed more often than that of Coke, nonetheless retains the signature blue, red and white colour combination.

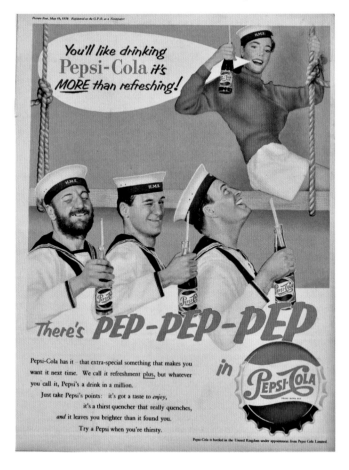

Persil takes its name from sodium perborate and silicate, the former a bleaching agent that made washing powder cost-effective and increased its market penetration. Düsseldorf manufacturer Henkel introduced Persil in 1907 and continues to make it, though Unilever now sells it in the UK.

PG Tips In the 1930s, Brooke Bond launched a tea in the UK under the name Pre-Gestee - a variant of its original name 'Digestive Tea'. The name implied that it could be drunk as a digestive aid prior to eating food. Grocers and salesmen abbreviated it to PG and this was subsequently adopted by the Company. The tea's name had another part added in 1950 to indicate that only the 'tips' of the tea plant were used. The long line of TV adverts featuring chimpanzees are still well-remembered.

Opposite: PG Tips advert from 1963.

Polo Mints Rowntree's marketing manager George Harris, who was the man behind some of the company's biggest brand names in the second half of the 1930s including KitKat, Smarties, Aero and Black Magic, had the idea for the mint around the same time but due to the second world war and sugar rationing it was shelved. However, Harris was determined to resurrect the idea and Polo mints first appeared in 1948. Before the war George had been inspired by the US brand Life Savers (a mint with a hole designed to look like a life-saving rubber ring) and had decided to make something similar in the UK. Company legend has it that he chose the name Polo because it derived from Polar and he thought that this implied the cool freshness of mint.

Porsche was founded in Stuttgart in 1930 by Dr Ferdinand Porsche, of Austrian birth. Under the National Socialist government, the company grew prominent through its design of the Volkswagen and its military offshoot, the Kübelwagen. Along the same lines came the Elefant tank destroyer of 1943. Whilst Ferdinand was imprisoned post-war, his son Ferry revitalised the company as a producer of high-performance racing cars, and products since then have all been of the highest cachet.

Prada were two brothers, Mario and Martino, who started a leather goods shop in Milan in 1913. Two further generations of Pradas had been in charge by the time concerted expansion into the high-end markets of Europe and the USA began in the 1980s, with the company's bags becoming particularly prized.

Premier Inn began as Travel Inn in 1987. Owners Whitbread bought Premier Lodge in 2004 and merged it with Travel Inn to form the current business under the name Premier Travel Inn, later shortened to Premier Inn.

Brooke Bond P.G.Tips
- tea you can really <u>taste</u>!

Pret a Manger, or 'ready to eat' plays on the fashion industry expression 'pret a porter' (ready to wear) and offers the same quick turnover of sandwiches, all made fresh with the surplus donated at the end of the day to the homeless. The first branch opened in London in 1983.

Opposite: Early 20th century advert for Quaker Oats.

Prezzo is simply Italian for Price, intentionally suggesting value. The first Prezzo restaurants were opened in this country in 2000.

Primark is a name invented for use on Penneys stores outside Ireland, where that brand was founded in 1969 and remains prominent; the Penneys name was otherwise trademarked by J.C. Penney, the large US department store chain. Widespread since introduction to the UK in 1973, Primark is able to hold costs down due to its lack of advertising, and now operates over 370 stores.

Primula Cheese Spread was developed in 1924 by Norwegian businessman Olav Kavli (1872–1958). It was the world's first spreadable processed cheese with a long shelf life and was named after the primula flower. The product was first introduced in the United Kingdom in 1929.

Pringles were created by Procter & Gamble and first appeared in parts of the US in 1967. They arrived in the UK in 1991 and are now owned by Kellogg's. Their designers reportedly used computers to ensure that the shape would keep them in place during packaging and that they would not break when being stacked. There are several theories behind the origin of the product's name. One theory refers to Mark Pringle, whose work was cited by P&G in filing their own patent for improving the taste of dehydrated potatoes.

Quaker Oats have no direct association with the Society of Friends, the Protestant Christian denomination; however, the industrious and responsible nature of the sect inspired one of the three partners in a US-Canadian consortium of oat mills, and the resulting friendly broad-hatted figure thus became the company symbol from 1877. The name was registered in the UK in 1894 and the cereal was first sold here in 1899. Porridge was once a staple food but is today a minor part of the breakfast cereal market.

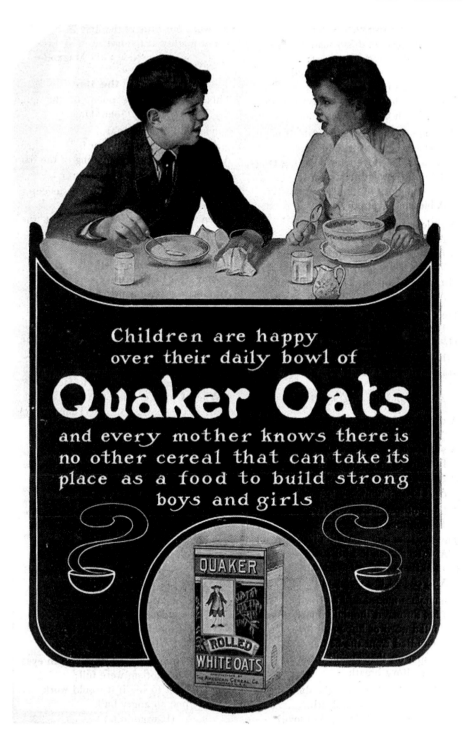

Quorn is a village in Leicestershire which gave its name to what is basically a fungus, grown as a meat replacement due to its high protein content. Marlow Foods, originally a consortium of Rank Hovis McDougall and ICI, developed the technique and first sold Quorn in the UK in 1993, expanding the line into vegetarian meals over the following decade and subsequently taking them to America and Australia.

Radox is short for 'radiate' and 'oxygen' and its first advertising slogan was 'radiates oxygen'. The bubble bath formula has been on sale in the UK since 1908.

Raleigh was set up in 1887 by Sir Frank Bowden, who had discovered a love for cycling after experiencing its health benefits first hand after a spell of bad health. The name comes from Raleigh Street in Nottingham, where the business's first factory was situated.

Range Rover was almost called Road Rover. The owning Rover company expanded upon the 'Rover' element of the rugged and versatile Land Rover to produce a larger and more luxurious vehicle. Prototypes appeared in 1967 and the Range Rover was launched in 1970, with four generations having followed.

Opposite: Cover of a Raleigh cycles brochure from 1951.

Ray-Ban simply 'bans rays'; its first sunglasses were developed in 1929 to reduce the effect of high-altitude sunlight on US Army pilots. Rochester, New York-based manufacturer Bausch & Lomb marketed the sunglasses and thus became a significant player in the optics market, whilst the shades themselves, in both round-lensed Aviator and horn-rimmed Wayfarer configuration, became associated with 'cool' through use in several films.

Red Bull Dietrich Mateschitz was an Austrian businessman who discovered a drink called Krathing Daeng during a sales trip to Hong Kong in 1982. It had been on sale there for about six years. He contacted Chaleo Yoovidhya, the creator of the drink, and they became business partners under a 'gentleman's agreement'. The product's name translates as Red Bull and by 1984 Red Bull was set up as a company poised to take a premium version of Krathing Daeng global. The two partners slightly reformulated Krathing Daeng for Western tastes and added carbonation.

Reebok is a name that dates from 1958 when the company was founded in England by a pair of brothers, Joe and Jeff Foster, to carry on a family tradition of making athletic footwear. Their grandfather, Joseph William Foster, had launched the J.W. Foster shoe company in 1895 and developed one of the very first track spikes. Joe and Jeff found 'rhebok' in a South African dictionary as a local name for a species of antelope that roamed the African continent. Inspired by the word, they changed the name of the company. Having expanded into athletic clothing in general, Reebok came into competition with Adidas and was bought by them in 2005.

Ribena derives from *ribes nigrum*, the Latin term for blackberries, the hot drink's key component. Introduced in 1938 by H.W. Carter of Bristol to push Vitamin C consumption among children in the absence of oranges, it was forever associated with comforting warming, although its sugar levels have been toned down in the last decade. At that point ownership passed from GlaxoSmithKline (heirs to Beecham) to Suntory of Japan.

RALEIGH

The All-Steel Bicycle
1951

for Luxury Cycling

Rolex The inventor of Rolex, Hans Wilsdorf, was looking to make an elegant, yet precise, wristwatch. He wanted a name that was easy to say, worked in different languages, and looked good on the watches. He settled on Rolex in 1908 as he thought that the name was onomatopoeic in sounding like a watch being wound.

Rolls-Royce, irrefutably British despite its handing down through several private and state concerns and ultimate takeover by BMW, combined, from 1904, the resources of Charles Rolls and Henry Royce. The latter's engineering skills were transferred seamlessly from crane production and ensured a high reputation, not only in hand-made cars but in iconic jet engines for aircraft.

Rowntree's In 1862 Henry Rowntree bought a cocoa works in York and, after his brother Joseph joined the company in 1869, developed it into a confectionery company. The brothers hired a French confectioner to develop the recipe for Rowntree's Fruit Pastilles, sold from 1881, which quickly established Rowntree's as a major brand. The brand is today owned by Nestlé.

Below: Ryvita advert from the 1930s.

Opposite: A 1950s Rowntree's advert.

Russell Hobbs began in 1952 when Bill Russell and Peter Hobbs teamed up to produce kitchen products in Britain. The first automatic electric kettle was one of their many innovations.

Ryanair takes its name from the surname of two of the three partners whose single turboprop aircraft began flying between Waterford and Gatwick in 1985. Air industry deregulation, EU expansion and a low-fares model (albeit with controversial on-board charges) propelled growth, as did early adoption of online booking that led to the phasing out of check-in desks.

Ryvita The Ryvita Company was established in 1925 by John Edwin Garratt, with a bakery set up in Birmingham two years later, producing one of the first packaged goods in the bakery field. The name combines its main ingredient Rye with Vitality.

Picture yourself in a pair of tights

RYVITA
makes you fit – keeps you slim

Sainsburys was established as a partnership in 1869, when John Sainsbury and his wife Mary opened a shop at 173 Drury Lane, London. Sainsbury started as a retailer of fresh foods and later expanded into packaged groceries such as tea and sugar and by 1903 had opened 100 shops. Its first self-service supermarket was opened in Croydon in 1950.

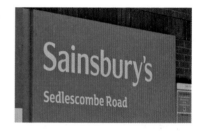

Samsung is Korean for 'three stars' and was founded in 1938. Its most significant field of electronics (particularly mobile phones and semiconductors) was ventured into from the 1960s, although its shipbuilding is now the world's second largest such concern. Mobile phones form the most visible indicator of company success and prominence today, having progressed from flat to innovative foldable forms.

Santander Bank began life as two separate building societies – The Abbey Road Building Society and the National Building Society, which merged in 1944. The Abbey Road company, which was the second biggest building society in the country at the time of the merger, dated back to 1874 when the 'Abbey Road and St John's Wood Permanent Benefit Building Society' was established. Abbey National became a bank in 1998. It was purchased by the Spanish Santander Bank in 2010 when the company also acquired the Bradford & Bingley Building Society. Santander is a city on the northern coast of Spain.

Schwartz, the spice company, was established in 1889 by William Schwartz, the son of a German immigrant to Canada. He convinced people it was better to buy pure, top quality spices in smaller quantities than poor quality bulk and began by travelling around Nova Scotia by bicycle selling his spices.

Schweppes Johann Schweppe, a watchmaker and amateur scientist, founded the Schweppes Company in Geneva in 1783 to sell carbonated water. Schweppe soon expanded the business from Geneva to England where consumers used the drink to settle upset stomachs. The company's fizzy water increased in popularity over the next fifty years and 'Schweppe's Aerated Lemon' (the first fizzy lemonade) was introduced in 1835 in the company's first move into flavoured drinks.

Scott's Porage Oats A. and R. Scott began producing Scott's Midlothian Oat Flour in 1880 in Glasgow, moving to Edinburgh in 1909, and the distinctive name Scott's Porage Oats was adopted in 1914. The company's unique spelling of porridge was a marketing trick: to distinguish themselves from their rivals, they combined the spellings of 'porridge' and 'potage' – a French word for a thick soup.

SEAT stands for the *Sociedad Española de Automóviles de Turismo* and is a Spanish car maker founded in May 1950 by *the Instituto Nacional de Industria (INI)*, a Spanish state-owned industrial holding company. The company entered the UK market in the 1980s.

Selfridges was founded by American Harry Gordon Selfridge with the opening of a store in Oxford Street in March 1909. Here, consumerism was taken to a high art with educational and scientific displays intended to make shopping a happier experience all round, akin to a leisure pursuit. Despite subsequent ownership by a variety of international concerns (John Lewis, followed by Sears), the flagship department store has remained an icon of Oxford Street and others operate in Birmingham and Manchester.

Sensodyne is a desensitising toothpaste for sensitive teeth that was launched in the US and UK in 1961. Its name comes from the words 'sensitive' and 'dyno', the latter short for 'dynamic'.

Sharwood's James Allen Sharwood was born in Islington, London, in 1859. Sharwood established himself as a wholesale grocer in Carter Lane from 1888 and Sharwood's Green Label mango chutney was introduced a year later. The company today produces many Indian, Chinese and South East Asian food products and ingredients as well as ready meals.

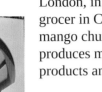

Shell is the trading name for Royal Dutch Shell plc, an amalgamation since 2005 of the long-standing Dutch and British legal entities that had been involved in petroleum extraction and exploitation since 1907. The recognisable logo, based on a giant scallop, harks back to the British arm of the organisation, whose founder's son gathered and sold Caspian Sea shells to collectors.

Siemens Werner von Siemens was an entrepreneur and inventor who played a key role in fostering the development of the electrical industry. His construction of the pointer telegraph laid the basis for his company Telegraphen-Bauanstalt von Siemens & Halske, founded in 1847 and soon to become an international enterprise. He had met Johann Georg Halske, a master mechanic, earlier that year. In 1866, Werner discovered the dynamo-electric principle, which helped to establish that electricity could be used as a power source.

Siri Technology inventor Dag Kittlaus named Siri after a co-worker in Norway, and it means 'beautiful woman who leads you to victory' in Norwegian. Siri's speech recognition engine was provided by Nuance Communications, a speech technology company, and developed for use by Apple who bought all the rights to Siri in 2010.

Skittles seem quintessentially American but actually started in Britain in 1974 before crossing the pond, being improved there and then sold back to us Brits. The small fruit-flavoured sweets with hard shells were imported into the USA in 1979 and produced there from 1982 by Wrigley's, now a subsidiary of Mars. It has been suggested that they were named after the balls used in the game of skittles.

Skoda The name of this car comes from founder Emil Škoda, who first built military equipment to help keep the Austro-Hungarian empire together at the turn of the 19th century. His company then merged with the bicycle works of the Laurin and Klement, in 1924, to pave the way for what the brand is today. Once a figure of fun in this country, the Skoda name is today used for quality cars produced by the VW group.

Skol, a Scandinavian word analogous to the English "Cheers!" has in reality little to do with Norse culture, the golden lager having been brewed in Alloa by Ind Coope breweries from 1958 and taking the name on sheer inspiration. Under the latter-day ownership of Carlsberg-Tetley's, which moved production to Leeds, Skol's alcohol content has been reduced to 2.8% to take advantage of that particular bracket of duty rates.

Sky, the upper reaches of where the titular satellites can be found, began in 1984 from Rupert Murdoch's long-held plans to introduce satellite broadcasting to the UK, but only really took off at the end of that decade when individual dishes and subscriptions replaced the provider model and outmanoeuvred cable TV in the process. Under a merger with British Satellite Broadcasting, the resulting BSkyB offered new and innovative programming and moved aggressively into broadcasting rights for football matches. Comcast acquired Sky in 2018.

Smarties The company's archivist says that there is no record of how, in 1937, the name Smarties was arrived at. Prior to the renaming these small sugar-coated chocolate sweets were called plain Chocolate Beans but were in all other respects the same product. The renaming and the advertising around it greatly increased demand. Within a year Smarties were so popular the firm had to build a new factory block solely for production of the sweets, and this had to be expanded again just a few months later.

Smeg was established in northern Italy in 1948 as a metal enamelling factory with the name *Smalterie Metallergiche Emiliane Guastalla*, giving it the present acronym of Smeg for its business of making a wide range of kitchen equipment. The company was introduced in the UK in 1989.

Snickers was the Mars family's favourite horse and in 1930 lent its name to a chocolate and caramel-covered peanut bar set in nougat. Even now, thirty years after the enforced adoption of the Snickers name, some aficionados of the identical UK-market product still refer to it under its former title, Marathon.

Sony is a shortened form of the company name in Japanese: *Sonī Kabushiki Kaisha*. This brand name may have been chosen for the audio-visual company's move into the global market as similar to the Latin word *sonus*, which is the root of sonic and sound. Sony Corporation was set up in 1958; its parent company dated back to 1946.

Sprite, a sort of energetic, ethereal variety of elf, was the name chosen by the Coca-Cola Company in 1960 to brand US-market sales of *Fanta Klare Zitrone* (Clear Lemon Fanta).

Stagecoach buses started in a small way in 1980 with an express coach service from Edinburgh to London using two secondhand coaches. One of the two coaches purchased had been given the name The Stage Coach, which led to brother and sister partnership Brian Souter and Ann Gloag using the name Stagecoach for their new business venture. The name comes from the long-distance horse-drawn stage coaches – so named because they operated long inter-city routes in stages between inns – until the new railways of the Victorian era killed them off. A journey from Manchester to London, for example, in the middle of the 18th Century took four and a half days in what was named a 'Flying Coach' to signify that it was a great improvement in speed to what had gone before.

Starburst, like Marathon becoming Snickers, was another enforced name change made to harmonise global marketing of identical products, but the British product, Opal Fruits, actually came first, introduced in 1960 by Wrigley. Even so, the Opal Fruits brand has been reintroduced twice since its deletion in 1998, both times as part of limited-edition promotions.

Stella Artois combines the name of Sébastian Artois, head brewer from 1708 at the Den Hoorn brewery in Leuven (or Louvain), Belgium, with the Christmas star, inspiration for a Christmas-themed pilsner first brewed in 1926 and soon expanded to year-round. The packaging, perfected by 1988 when Brouwerij Artois joined the Interbrew consortium, fuses the horn of Den Hoorn and its founding date (1366) with a motif based on the architecture of Leuven.

Strongbow was the alleged nickname of Richard de Clare, 2nd Earl of Pembroke, who used bowmen to invade Ireland in 1172. H.P. Bulmer, already pre-eminent in cider brewing, thus named a line in 1960 and propelled it to widespread popularity within just ten years. Bulmers is now owned by Heineken.

Superdry apparel evokes Japanese culture but is purely British, having first appeared in 2003. The founders, who before teaming up had been selling skatewear for the previous decade and a half, were inspired by the 'super' appellation they saw on multiple Japanese products when visiting Tokyo.

Swatch watches first appeared in 1983 as a Swiss-made analogue counter to Japanese digital watches' popularity. They were designed to be so cheap they could be anyone's 'second watch', and were developed with a sense of fun and fashion that facilitated their popularity. Growth was such that the resulting Swatch group was able, over time, to purchase several established competitors like Longines, Omega and Tissot.

Tarmac is a name formed from 'tar' and the surname of John Loudon McAdam, who devised the durable surface material made up of tar and small broken stones. It is properly called Tarmacadam but is usually abbreviated to Tarmac.

Tate & Lyle is named after Henry Tate and Abram Lyle, two fierce competitors in sugar refining whose businesses dated from 1859 and 1865 respectively. The former invented sugar cubes and the latter Golden Syrup. Their companies merged in 1921, after both had died, to form Tate & Lyle. Henry Tate founded the Tate Gallery on Millbank in 1897.

1898 advert for
Golden Syrup.

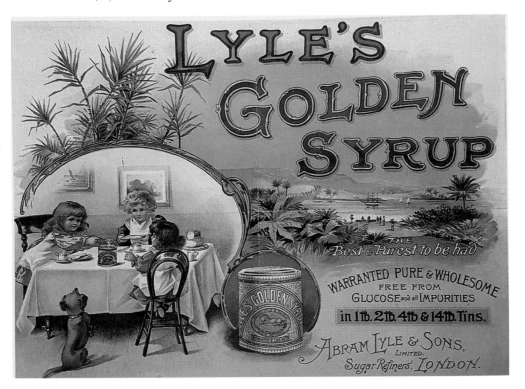

Teapigs were created in 2006 and innovated by designing mesh teabags (or 'tea temples') into which whole leaf tea could be placed for maximum distillation. The name was coined, the founders explain, because they were "just greedy for great tea!"

Ted Baker, like Mr Kipling and Uncle Ben, is a fictional character – in this case dreamed up by founder Ray Kelvin in case he had to separate himself from the brand (which is just what has happened more recently). The luxury clothing business was launched in Glasgow in 1988.

Teflon comes from chemical name polytetrafluoroethylene with the arbitrary ending -on and was introduced as a coating for non-stick pans in the 1960s.

Tesco Made up from the initials of T. E. Stockwell and the first two letters of the supermarket chain's founder Jack Cohen's surname. T. E. Stockwell was a tea importer and the name Tesco was first used in 1924 for a brand of tea, later becoming the name used for Cohen's first shop, which opened in 1929 at Burnt Oak near Edgware. The company's first self-service store opened in St Albans in 1948.

Tetley Tea In 1822, brothers Joseph and Edward Tetley sold salt from a pack horse in Huddersfield. They then started to sell tea and were so successful they set up as Joseph Tetley & Company tea merchants in 1837.

Tetley's Brewery coincidentally also has its origins in 1822, when Tetley's Brewery was founded by Joshua Tetley in Hunslet, near Leeds. By 1860 Tetley was the largest brewery in the North of England.

Tiffany was established in New York in 1837 by Charles Lewis Tiffany, originally as a stationery and gift shop. The three later partners went into jewellery making almost by accident but soon became prominent in the field and Tiffany stores soon appeared in Paris and London. The company's signature blue came about from the colour on the cover of its first catalogue in 1845 and, helped by the perceived rarity of turquoise gemstones, gradually developed into their familiar robin's-egg shade.

Tilda was founded in London in the early 1970s. The company's name is a combination from the names of the founder's daughters Tila and Daksha. The company introduced Pure Basmati rice in large bags to rice-loving communities from around the world, who were looking for the aromatic Basmati they couldn't find in the UK at the time.

Tiptree The Tiptree jam story begins at the time when William Gladstone was Prime Minister in the second half of the 19th Century. When he commended fruit preserving to the population at large, Arthur Charles Wilkin leapt on this idea as a way to make a success of farming in the Essex village of Tiptree. In 1885, The Britannia Fruit Preserving Company was formed and the very first 'Tiptree' preserves were made.

TK Maxx, as distinct from its US parent TJ Maxx, came to the UK in 1994 with the subtle name change imposed to avoid confusion with T.J. Hughes, a similar apparel company. There are now over five hundred stores in the UK.

Toblerone's distinctive shape owes itself to Theodor Tobler, a Swiss confectioner allegedly inspired by the shape of the Matterhorn. His cousin and business partner Emil Baumann came up with the chocolate. The first bars were made in 1908 and the manufacturing process trademarked in 1909, but, as with most food concerns, ownership has passed through a series of hands in more recent years; Tobler and Suchard merged in 1970, then joined up with Jacobs in 1982 and in 1990 all three were bought by Kraft Foods, forerunner of today's Mondelez.

Topshop started as Peter Robinson's Top Shop, an offshoot of a women's fashion chain that had already been acquired by Burton. Positioned as a high fashion youth brand, it quickly eclipsed the Peter Robinson name and by the 1980s was attracting trendy designers to produce capsule collection. Topman was simultaneously established to usher men's tailoring into the modern era.

Toyota was founded in 1926 as Toyoda Automatic Loom Works, which produced an innovative loom, but engine production commenced in 1933 with the name subtly modified to Toyota, which could be written in eight calligraphic strokes, a lucky number in Japan (Toyoda requires ten). Passenger cars followed in 1936 but it wasn't until the 1970s that US and European market penetration was achieved, the small, reliable and fuel-efficient models helping to fend off the oil crisis. The modern badge was devised in 1989 and consists of three ovals forming the letter T for Toyota.

Tupperware was invented by Earl Tupper, who introduced the first sales in 1946. He was an American so Earl was his name, not his title. Tupper, a chemist, was experimenting with plastic which, back then, was new and unpopular.

Twinings Tea was founded by Thomas Twining, of Painswick, Gloucestershire, who opened Britain's first known tea room, at 216 Strand, London, in 1706; it still operates today. The firm's logo, created in 1787, is the world's oldest in continuous use. It is now the best-selling tea brand in Britain, having overtaken PG Tips in 2019.

Twitter Having rejected the name Twitch for their social networking service, co-founder Jack Dorsey says: "We looked in the dictionary for words around it and came across the word 'twitter,' and it was just perfect". The definition was "a short burst of inconsequential information". And that's exactly what the product was about.

Typhoo Tea is named after the Chinese word for doctor and was first sold in the UK in 1903. It was originally named Typhoo Tipps because the stalk of the tea leaf was cut off to remove the tannins that could cause indigestion. It was advertised as the tea that doctors recommend. When introduced it was normal for tea to be sold loose over the counter in plain bags. Typhoo was the first pre-packaged and branded tea.

Twix is a comparatively recent introduction despite its ubiquity and popularity, appearing in 1967 as 'twin sticks' (hence the name) covered with caramel and chocolate. Unusually, corporate harmonisation has favoured the British product this time, with the European version ditching its Raider name for Twix between 1991 and 2000.

UGG Boots is a trademark for a kind of sheepskin boot pioneered in Australia and renowned for being, in the opinion of the wife of one of the earliest manufacturers, 'ugly'. Profits are quite the opposite, however, the trademarked product (founded in California in 1978 and acquired by Deckers in 1995) having racked up billion-dollar sales.

Uncle Ben – as he appears on packets of rice – was in fact a man called Frank Brown, a maître d'hôtel at a Chicago restaurant in the mid-1950s. The restaurant was frequented by Gordon L. Harwell who approached Frank to have a portrait painted for use on his packets of pre-cooked rice. The Uncle Ben brand was born.

Underground The word Underground, for London's tube network, was adopted at a conference of what were then separate underground railway companies in February 1908. It was one of three names considered, the other two being 'the Tube' and 'the Electric'. None of them was ideal. A minority of the network of lines was underground, true now as it was then, and deep-level tube tunnels were also in the minority. All of the lines taking part were electric powered but then so were the trams that ran in the streets above. 'Underground' was chosen as the least-worst option. The modern tendency to refer to the whole network as 'the Tube' overlooks the shallow 'cut and cover' lines with larger profile tunnels and trains that are not in tubes. This compounds the way the word Underground overlooks the 55% or so of the network that is on the surface.

United Colours of Benetton In 1969 brothers Luciana and Carlo Benetton opened their first Benetton clothing store in Belluno, a town in Italy, and three years after in Paris. The advertising slogan United Colours of Benetton arrived in 1985 with posters showing people with flags of different countries and this slogan became the company's brand in 1989.

Uniqlo, or Unique Clothing Warehouse, takes its abbreviation from a spelling mistake that used a Q in place of a C in documentation from the 1984-founded Japanese casual-wear stores. Sales spread through imitation of The Gap's strategy to manufacture its own products and use low-cost Chinese labour to do so. Over 2000 stores now operate worldwide.

Vaseline In the 1860s, Robert Chesebrough, a chemist from New York, discovered Petroleum Jelly. In 1870, this product was branded as Vaseline Petroleum Jelly and by 1875 Americans were buying it at the rate of a jar a minute. It got its brand name from the German for water (*wasser*) and the Greek for oil (*elaion*) after Chesebrough's work purifying the petroleum oil so that, like water, it was colourless and odourless. The company was purchased by Unilever in 1987.

Vauxhall is the UK badge for Opel cars, both for a very long time subsidiaries of General Motors until sale to Groupe PSA in 2017. Origins were in steam-powered engines for river boats, first produced in 1857 at Alexander Wilson and Company's works in Vauxhall, south-west London, and proceeding from there to cranes, petrol engines and, by the end of the 19th century, cars.

Velcro In 1948, Swiss engineer and amateur mountaineer George de Mestral went hiking in the woods with his dog. Upon arriving back at his home, he took note of the burrs that clung to his clothes and he wondered if such an idea could be useful in commercial application. He studied a burr under a microscope only to discover that they were covered in tiny hooks, which allowed them to grab onto clothes and fur that brushed in passing. After some years of research and work, he created what is known today as Velcro, a combination of the words 'velvet' and 'crochet.' He patented Velcro in 1955.

Verizon, the telecommunications company, was founded in New Jersey in 2000. The name combines the Latin word *veritas*, meaning truth, with the word horizon.

Vesta is the Roman goddess of the hearth, home and family and her name was used for the brand of ready made meals introduced in 1962.

Victoria's Secret was what founder Roy Raymond imagined the eponymous Queen might be wearing underneath her otherwise staid robes; the lingerie store, first opened in Palo Alto, California in 1977, was envisaged as friendly to males purchasing for their significant others and the strategy paid off, aided by the iconic catalogue and catwalk fashion shows. Less significant in recent times, the company's UK arm entered administration in 2020.

Vimto is another soft drink produced as a health tonic, in this case capable of giving you 'vim'. First bottled in Manchester in 1908 by John Noel Nichols, Vim Tonic was soon contracted to Vimto.

Virgin The first Virgin Records shop was opened by Richard Branson in Oxford Street in 1971 after he had earlier established a mail order record business. Branson's Virgin brand grew rapidly during the 1980s as he started his Virgin Atlantic airline and Virgin Records music label. The choice for his company name started as a bit of a joke. According to the company there were a number of contenders, including 'Slipped Disc.' But then someone suggested Virgin, as they were all virgins at business. As the company tells it, they all laughed but the name was chosen.

Visa derives from the Latin *charta visa* ('paper that has been seen') and since 1976 has been the name of BankAmericard, a credit card introduced in 1958 in the US and competing ever since then with what is now Mastercard. The name and its attendant blue and yellow house colours were introduced to unify a disparate system of multiple licensees, and more recently has been a holding name for a range of debit cards.

Vodafone, or 'voice, data, fone', came out of a deal struck by Racal Electronics in 1980 to license GEC's tactical battlefield radio for commercial applications. The resulting Racal Telecom became more valuable than its holding group and was demerged in 1991 as Vodafone Group. It was early into consumer mobile phones as they became widespread during the 1990s, gaining strength by merging and acquiring. Side ventures into motorsport and football shirt sponsorship underscored the brand's market penetration.

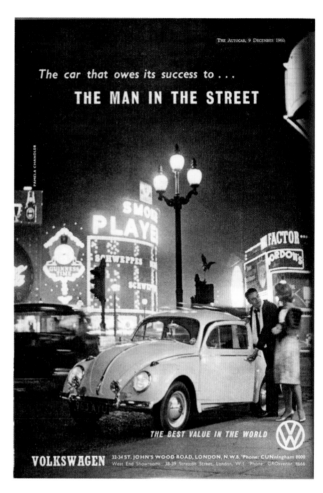

The Autocar, 9 December 1960.

The car that owes its success to . . .

THE MAN IN THE STREET

Volkswagen (VW) began as a Nazi prestige project in 1934. Adolf Hitler and Ferdinand Porsche were the people behind the company's first mass-produced "people's car", the beetle-shaped *Kraft-durch-Freude-Wagen* ('Strength Through Joy Car', usually abbreviated to *KdF-Wagen),* introduced in 1937. After the second world war the company, partly under British direction, became part of Germany's post-war economic boom and Beetle production increased. In the 1970s came the birth of a new generation of Volkswagens with the Passat, Scirocco, Golf and Polo models.

THE BEST VALUE IN THE WORLD

VOLKSWAGEN 32-34 ST. JOHN'S WOOD ROAD, LONDON, N.W.8. 'Phone: CUNningham 8000
West End Showrooms: 38-39 Stratton Street, London, W.1. 'Phone: GROsvenor 4666

Volvo, the Latin for 'I roll', was established in 1915 by Gothenburg ball-bearing manufacturer SKF but the Volvo name christened the company's first cars in 1927. Designed to withstand the harsh Swedish climate, Volvo cars gained a reputation for toughness and safety.

W.H. Smith was the name of the second and third generation of London news vendors established since 1792. William Henry Smith and son expanded on to early railway station platforms during the railway boom of the mid-19th century and diversified into a library and publishing business, which in the 20th century added 'Do It All' DIY stores, Our Price record shops and, for a ten-year period, Waterstone's.

Wagamama roughly translates as self-indulgent, self-centred, selfish, disobedient or wilful and is most often used in Japan to describe a badly behaved child. The food in this chain of eating places arrives as soon as it is ready, so diners are not expected to wait for others before they tuck-in. The first branch opened in London's Bloomsbury in 1992.

Wahaca is a phonetic spelling of the south-western Mexican state of Oaxaca, a name used for a UK restaurant group selling Mexican-style street food, co-founded by Thomasina Miers. The first branch opened in London in 2007.

Waitrose conflates two of the founders' surnames, Wallace Waite and Arthur Rose, the title having been coined when the third partner, David Taylor, left the small grocery in 1908, four years after its opening in Acton. By 1937 there were ten stores, at which point the John Lewis Partnership took over, but concerted expansion to the level of today (over 330 stores) commenced only in the 1980s. A rebranding in 2003 took the brand consciously upmarket.

Walkers crisps Walkers was founded in 1948 in Leicester by Henry Walker. Today, the Walkers plant in Leicester is the largest crisp production plant in the world, producing over 11 million bags of crisps per day and using about 800 tons of potatoes. The previous brand leader in crisps, Smith's, was purchased by Walkers in 1989 and the name discontinued.

TAKE HOME SOME WALL'S – FOR THE JOY IT GIVES !

Wall's was founded in 1786 by Richard Wall when he opened a butcher's stall in St James's Market, London. Wall died in 1838 and was succeeded by his widow, and then his son, Thomas Wall, born in 1817. Thomas Wall Jr became partner from 1870. He was joined by his brother Frederick C. Wall from 1878 and the firm became known as Thomas Wall & Sons. Thomas and Frederick Wall transformed the firm into the best-known sausage business in Britain. In 1913, Thomas wanted to move into a refreshing snack for hot summer days and in what the company describes as a Eureka moment he decided to add ice cream to the company's offering. The first world war delayed the start of this but ice cream production commenced in 1922 at a factory in Acton.

Part of a Wall's advert from the late 1950s.

Opposite: a Weetabix advert from about the same time.

Warburtons is a British baking firm founded in Bolton by Thomas Warburton in 1876. For much of its history Warburtons had bakeries in Lancashire only, being slow to spread to other parts of northern England and then the rest of Britain. It remains a family-owned company.

Waterstones was founded by Tim Waterstone in 1982 with the intention of building a chain of bookshops with a wide specialist range, friendly atmosphere to browse in and knowledgeable booksellers. The first branch was opened in Old Brompton Road, London. Tim sold the business in 1993. It nicely retains a very British image, though is currently owned by the American investment company Elliott Management Corporation, who bought it from a Russian billionaire in 2011 for $683m.

WD-40 Persistence paid off when the chemist who was attempting in 1953 to concoct a formula to prevent corrosion – a task that's done by displacing water – finally succeeded on his 40th try. His creation, WD-40, literally stands for Water Displacement 40th formula. Despite its original use, WD-40 is now employed for everything from silencing squeaky hinges to removing road tar from cars.

Weetabix is the British variant, since 1932, of the Australian cereal product Weet-Bix which continues there under the original name. Both describe 'wheat biscuits'. The lozenge-shaped pressed products have featured in animated TV adverts during the 1980s and more recently parodying Jack and the Beanstalk. A spin-off product introduced in 2006 used oats and was therefore called Oatibix.

Westfield The Westfield Group had origins in the western suburbs of Sydney. The first shopping centre development was named Westfield Place and opened there in July 1959. The name Westfield is related to the West Sydney location together with 'field' due to its being built there on old farmland. The first Westfield shopping centre in Britain opened in 2008 at Shepherd's Bush, west London.

Whirlpool In 1908, Lou Upton of Michigan, US, invested his savings in a venture to manufacture household equipment. When that company failed, Upton was offered the opportunity to select something of value from the failed venture as a return on his investment. He chose the patents on a hand washing machine that he thought might be electrified, beginning production in 1911 under the name Upton Machine Company. Whirlpool was later chosen as the brand name for its washing machines and this became the company's official name from 1949.

Whole Earth In 1967 brothers Craig and Gregory Sams opened an organic, vegetarian, macrobiotic restaurant in London called Seeds – a pioneering move, when you consider that organic food was little-known back then. They went on to create Whole Earth, a company that would bring organic food to the masses – everything from peanut butter to the UK's first organic cornflakes. Part of their aim was to do their bit to make the earth whole again, hence the name.

Wickes opened its first UK store in 1972 but had traded in the USA since 1854 when Henry Dunn Wickes started a lumber plant in Michigan. Consolidating building and materials into a one-stop shop was what drove success and the inspiration to spread abroad, and the DIY craze that flourished in Britain at that point established the brand here in a fierce field of competitors. Under the aegis of Travis Perkins (since 2004), Wickes currently boasts over 230 stores and plans are afoot to spin it off into a self-standing business.

Wilkinson Sword is a company with origins dating back to the 1770s, when a Henry Nock began selling guns and bayonets. When Nock died in 1804, he left the company to his foreman and adopted son-in-law James Wilkinson, and when his son Henry joined the company it was renamed James Wilkinson & Son. The company became the Wilkinson Sword Company in 1891. Seven years later the company produced its first shaving product – the 'Pall Mall' safety razor.

Wilko became such a popular abbreviation of Wilkinson's among its customers that the company has adopted it as its own new name. James Kemsey Wilkinson opened a hardware shop in Leicester in 1930 and had nine by the end of the decade. The modern operation is very much like the old Woolworth's, with the main effort being in value-for-money own-brand household products.

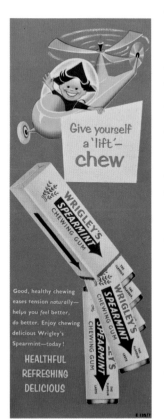

Give yourself
a 'lift'–
chew

Good, healthy chewing
eases tension *naturally*—
helps you *feel* better,
do better. Enjoy chewing
delicious Wrigley's
Spearmint—today !

HEALTHFUL
REFRESHING
DELICIOUS

Wrigley's William Wrigley Jr was born in Philadelphia in 1861. His company, Wrigley's, was originally a maker of soap and baking soda in Chicago. Founded by him in 1891, the company offered customers free packs of chewing gum with every purchase. He was to discover that the gum was actually more popular than the products it was promoting, and so chewing gum became the focus of his business. Wrigley's Spearmint gum went on sale in Britain in 1911.

Xerox comes from the Greek word *xeros* meaning dry and *graphos* relating to something drawn or written. The Xerox company has its origins in the Haloid Company founded in 1906. In 1949 it produced its first Xerox dry photocopier, which became so successful that the company's name was changed to Haloid Xerox in 1958 and subsequently to Xerox Corporation.

Xylitol derives from Ancient Greek xyl[on], 'wood', with the suffix -itol used to denote sugar alcohols. The product is a made from a naturally occurring alcohol found in most plant material, including many fruits and vegetables. It is widely used as a sugar substitute and in sugar-free chewing gums, mints and other sweets. The name was registered as a trade mark in 2009.

Yahoo (suffixed at first with an exclamation mark) was an easier-to-remember name than 'Jerry and David's Guide to the World Wide Web', a hierarchical index of the burgeoning Internet compiled in 1994 by Jerry Yang and David Filo, two Stanford graduate students. As well as being an exclamation in its own right, a yahoo is also a rude creature in Jonathan Swift's *Gulliver's Travels*, a work that inspired the founders. Yahoo became its own empire in the space of a decade, but was outmanoeuvred in pure search by Google and failed to maintain control over later innovations like mobile telcoms and social media; since 2017 it has been just a small part of Verizon.

Yellow Pages is, contrary to popular opinion, not a registered trademark and nor is the 'let your fingers do the walking' graphic designed by AT&T. The concept came about quite by accident when a Cheyenne, Wyoming printer of telephone directories, growing in popularity by 1883, ran out of white paper and had to substitute yellow. The colour remained distinct as a way to differentiate businesses from residential numbers and the Yellow Pages name made its way into modern Internet search functions as Yell, launched in the UK in 1996.

Yodel is a parcels company in the United Kingdom, originally known as the Home Delivery Network until rebranding in 2010. The name is short for Your Deliveries.

Yorkie This chocolate bar was launched by Rowntree's in 1976 and named after the city in which the factory that produces it is situated. Rowntree's was purchased by Nestlé in 1988 but the chocolate bar continues to be produced in York.

Yorkshire Tea was launched – perhaps surprisingly recently – in 1977 with the idea of producing tea to suit the local water. It is a product of the merger of Taylors, in being since 1886, with Betty's Tea Rooms of Harrogate to produce Bettys & Taylors Group. The brand is advertised as being as rugged and down-to-earth as Yorkshire itself. In the early days of the company different blends were created and sold for different regions of Yorkshire according to variations in the hardness or softness of the water. It soon won the loyalty of tea drinkers farther afield – both across the UK and even worldwide.

Zanussi The Zanussi Company began in 1916 as a small workshop owned by Antonio Zanussi, the 26-year-old son of a blacksmith in Pordenone in north-eastern Italy. He began the business by making home stoves and wood-burning ovens. It continues to produce ovens today, together with washing machines and dryers. The company entered the UK market in the 1970s and was taken over by Electrolux in 1984.

Zara Amancio Ortega opened the first Zara store in 1975 in Coruña, Spain. He initially named the store Zorba after the classic film *Zorba the Greek*, but after learning there was a bar with the same name two blocks away he changed it to Zara, probably unaware that when used in English speaking countries as a girl's first name it means 'princess' – a happy coincidence for a woman's clothing store chain.

Bibliography

How it all Began up the High Street   Maurice Baren
Michael O'Mara Books, London, 1996

How Household Names Began   Maurice Baren
Michael O'Mara Books, London, 1997

Packaging Source Book Robert Opie
Little, Brown, London, 1989

Remember When   Robert Opie
Mitchell Beazley, London, 1999

Sweet Memories   Robert Opie
Pavilion Books, London, 1999

The Secret History of Brands   Matt MacNabb
Pen & Sword, Barnsley, 2017

Acknowledgements
Thanks to Alamy, Five Starr Photos, 'Steve' and Leah O'Carroll
for illustrations.